119446

Romans

A Verse by Verse Study

ROMANS

A Verse by Verse Study

Herschel H. Hobbs

WORD BOOKS, PUBLISHER

Waco, Texas

Romans: A Verse by Verse Study

Copyright © 1977 by Word, Incorporated, Waco, Texas.

All rights reserved.

Library of Congress catalog card number: 76–48547
ISBN 0–87680–513–6

Printed in the United States of America

For information on Scripture versions used, see p. 6.

To All Who Proclaim
the God-Kind-of-Righteousness

The following Scripture versions are used or referred to in the text:

NAS   *New American Standard Bible* © The Lockman Foundation 1960, 1962, 1963, 1968, 1971

ASV   The American Standard Version, 1901

RSV   The Revised Standard Version of the Bible, copyrighted 1946, 1952, © 1971, 1973 by the Division of Christian Education of the National Council of the Churches of Christ in the U.S.A., used by permission.

NEB   *The New English Bible,* © The Delegates of The Oxford University Press and The Syndics of The Cambridge University Press 1961, 1970, used by permission.

TEV   Today's English Version of the New Testament (*Good News for Modern Man*), copyright © American Bible Society 1966.

Beck   *The New Testament in the Language of Today* by William F. Beck. Copyright © 1963 by Concordia Publishing House.

Berkeley   *The Holy Bible, The Berkeley Version in Modern English* by Gerrit Verkuyl. The New Testament, copyright © 1945 by Zondervan Publishing House.

Conybeare   *The Epistles of Paul* by W. J. Conybeare, Wm. B. Eerdman's Pub. Co.

Goodspeed   *The New Testament: An American Translation* by Edgar J. Goodspeed, copyright © 1923, 1948 by the University of Chicago.

Knox   *The Holy Bible. Translated by Ronald Knox.* Copyright © 1944, 1948, 1950 by Sheed & Ward, Inc.

Moffatt   *The New Testament: A New Translation* by James Moffatt, copyright © 1964 by James Moffatt, published by Harper & Row, Inc.

Montgomery   *The Centenary Translation: The New Testament in Modern English,* translated by Helen Barrett Montgomery, copyright © 1924, 1952 by the American Baptist Board of Education and Publication, published by Judson Press.

Phillips   *The New Testament in Modern English* by J. B. Phillips, © 1958, 1960, 1972 by J. B. Phillips, published by The Macmillan Company.

Rotherham   *The Emphasized New Testament* by Joseph Bryant Rotherham, Kregel Publications.

    The Twentieth Century New Testament, Moody Press.

Weymouth   *The New Testament in Modern Speech* by Richard Francis Weymouth, Harper & Row.

Williams   *The New Testament: A Translation in the Language of the People* by Charles B. Williams, copyright © 1937 by Bruce Humphries, Inc., copyright © renewed 1965 by Edith S. Williams, Moody Press.

Contents

Introduction

In the closing sentence of his introduction to *Romans* (the Broadman Bible Commentary, volume 10), Dale Moody says, "There will never be a definitive commentary on Romans, for the well is too deep to run dry, so that all may still come to this fountain to renew faith." This statement explains why with so many other works on Romans this effort to write another is made. As will be evident from reading this volume, no effort is made toward novelty or to deal with questions raised by various interpreters. My purpose is to endeavor to interpret Romans in terms of the needs of pastors and laymen who may or may not be versed in such questions. This has been the overriding purpose in all of my attempts at written exposition of various New Testament books. To use electronic terms, my hope is to take the *current* of the epistle off the high tension line and transform it down to the voltage of general and practical use. Where textual problems exist they will be pointed out, but my primary desire is to let the message come through in such a manner as to make it useful in preaching, teaching, and daily living.

Moody (pp. 159–60) also notes how through the Christian era Romans has been at the center of various renewals of the faith set forth in the New Testament. He quotes from Anders Nygren's *Commentary on Romans:* "The history of the Christian church is consequently witness to the fact that the Epistle to the Romans has in a peculiar way been able to supply the impulse for the renewal of Christianity. When man has slipped away from the gospel, a deep study of Romans has often been the means by which the lost has been recovered" (p. 3).

I make no claim that this is a "deep study" of Romans, but perhaps it will reach, encourage, and challenge those to whom it is primarily directed. That we need a "renewal of Christianity" today is quite evident. "Grievous wolves" from without the Christian fellowship "enter in . . . not sparing the flock. Also of [*ek,* out of] your own selves . . . men arise, speaking perverse things, to draw away disciples after them" (Acts 20:29–30). Let others strike out at these with their heavy artillery if they will, but rifle fire must also be heard as the ground troops move in to possess and secure the area. As one of the foot soldiers of the cross, having spent almost a half-century in the pastorate, this work is my rifle in the fray.

9

Authorship, Date, and Place of Writing

That the author of Romans is the Apostle Paul is established with few questioning voices. Assuming that the epistle was written from Corinth, though a few suggest Philippi soon after Paul left Corinth, it was probably written shortly before he went to Jerusalem at the end of his third missionary journey (Rom. 15:19–29). It is possible that he also wrote Galatians just prior to Romans. They deal with the same general theme, although it is more fully presented in Romans.

The focal date in Pauline chronology is the term of Gallio as proconsul of Achaia in A.D. 51, probably beginning in July of that year (Acts 18:12–17). This date is derived from an inscription at Delphi which preserves a letter from Claudius Caesar in which he refers to Gallio as proconsul. It is not known how long after Gallio arrived in Corinth that Paul was brought before him or how long Paul remained in the city after that event. Paul's ministry in Corinth lasted about eighteen months. From the account in Acts it is possible that the appearance before Gallio came early in the period. Assuming that this was sometime in A.D. 51, and allowing for Paul's visit to Jerusalem for the Passover, followed by his extended ministry in Ephesus (Acts 19), we come to Paul's three-month ministry in Corinth (Acts 20:3). This probably was in late A.D. 56 and early 57. Paul was in Philippi at the time of the Passover. He wanted to arrive in Jerusalem by Pentecost (Acts 20:16).

If he wrote Romans shortly before leaving Corinth, which seems reasonable, it would place the date of writing in the late winter or early spring of A.D. 57.

The Church in Rome

In all probability there was a Christian church in Rome prior to Paul's coming to Europe (Acts 16:11–12). In A.D. 49 Claudius expelled the Jews from Rome. Among them were Aquila and Priscilla who met Paul upon his first arrival in Corinth (Acts 18:2). They were Jewish Christians with a mature faith (Acts 18:26). In his biography of Claudius, Suetonius says, "Since the Jews were continually making disturbances at the instigation of Chrestus, he [Claudius] expelled them from Rome." *Chrestus* apparently is the Latin spelling of *Christus*. So the Jews of Rome—there were probably about forty thousand of them—evidently opposed the preaching about Christ. The early church in Rome was no doubt predominantly Jewish although later it was made up largely of Gentile Christians. But it is evident that this church existed for some time prior to A.D. 49. Who founded the church in Rome? Moody (p. 154) quotes from an anonymous writer, whom Erasmus called Ambrosiaster, to the effect that the Romans "had embraced the faith of Christ, albeit according to the Jewish rite, without any sign of mighty works or any of the apostles." Conservative Roman Catholicism, on the basis of statements of Eusebius and Jerome that Peter came to Rome at the beginning of the reign of Claudius (A.D. 41–54), sees Peter as the founder. However, recent Roman Catholic biblical scholars agree with Protestantism that this is doubtful.

According to Clement of Rome in his letter to the Corinthians (A.D. 95), Peter later came to Rome and died there. This point is strengthened if one assumes that Peter's use of "Babylon" (1 Pet. 5:13) is symbolic of Rome as is true in Revelation (14:8; 17:5). Clement also speaks of Paul as "having taught righteousness to the whole world [Roman Empire], even reaching the bounds of the west [Spain]," and that he "left the world and went to the holy place." In all likelihood both Peter and Paul perished in the Neronic persecution of A.D. 64–68.

However, the point of all this is that neither Peter nor Paul founded the church in Rome. Paul's stated ambition to preach the gospel where no other had laid the foundation, rules against an apostolic origin of this church (Rom. 15:20). Of course, his primary reference here is to Spain (v. 24). On his journey there he wishes also to visit Rome. It seems, therefore, that the church in Rome was founded by Christians such as Aquila and Priscilla who had gone there from other parts of the empire.

The Purpose of Romans

Paul had many friends in Rome (Rom. 16). It is natural that many with whom he had worked elsewhere would go to the capital city of the empire. This would be added incentive for the apostle to make a visit to Rome on his way to Spain. Following the death of Claudius, many Jews evidently had returned to Rome (Acts 28:17–29).

For the most part the Christians in Rome had never heard Paul preach; so in anticipation of his visit there he wrote what became the Book of Romans in which he set forth the gospel as he had preached it. For this reason we have in this letter the most complete statement of the gospel found in the New Testament. It is, therefore, understandable why this epistle has figured so prominently in spiritual renewal through the centuries.

The theme of Romans is God's righteousness (see Rom.

1:17). Or it may be designated as *The God-Kind-of-Righteous-ness*. *Righteousness* (*dikaiosunē*) and *justification* (*dikaiōma, dikaiōsis*) render Greek words which belong to the same family of words. The verb form *dikaioō* means to make right or just. In the judicial sense it means to declare a person righteous or just. Thus the substantives (nouns) depict these states of being declared righteous or justified before God.

The God-kind-of-righteousness is based upon the gracious act of God in Christ. It is not *achieved* in terms of good works, but is *received* through faith in Jesus Christ (see Rom. 3:20–24). Another way of stating the theme of Romans is *justification by faith*. And, of course, this involves God's grace. This theme needs emphasis today as it did in the first century.

In this work the basic text followed is the King James Version; I have indicated when other translations are used, and full information on them is given on page 6. For clarity at times I will translate directly from the Greek text. In the desire for simplicity, authors from whom I have quoted are cited by name and page number. Complete reference information on these works and other related materials is given in the bibliography.

1

The Introduction to the Epistle

Romans 1:1–18

When Paul began dictating Romans to Tertius (Rom. 16:22), it is unlikely that he knew he was producing one of the greatest religious documents ever written or that it would bear so great an influence upon the cause of Christ through the centuries. His primary purpose was to acquaint his readers with the gospel of Christ as he had preached it around the eastern circle of the Mediterranean. Furthermore, he wished to counteract the false teachings of the Judaizers (Rom. 15:8–16; 16:17–19).

The Judaizers were Jewish Christians, former Pharisees (see Acts 15:5), who insisted that in order to be saved Gentiles must first become Jews in religion and then believe in Jesus. To become Jewish proselytes Gentiles would have to be circumcised and then live by the Mosaic law. After the Jerusalem Council in A.D. 49 (see Acts 15; Gal. 2) ruled against the Judaizers in favor of Paul and his gospel of grace through faith, they continued to harass him, attacking his apostleship, person, character, and message. They were more active in Galatia, as is seen in Galatians which probably was written from Corinth just before Romans. Whether or not the Judaizers had reached Rome at this time is not clear, but the apostle places the Romans on guard against them.

Paul was aware that he wrote under the inspiration of the Holy Spirit (Rom. 16:25). Even so, he could not foresee the future effect of this writing. However, Christianity is debtor beyond measure for this work from the heart and mind of the greatest of all the interpreters of Christ and the gospel. Out of this sense of debtorship to share the gospel we approach this study of Romans.

The Signature, Address, and Greeting (1:1–7)

Paul opened this epistle in his typical fashion in keeping with the Greek practice of the time. He began by signing the letter; then he addressed it and extended a greeting. He modified the details from time to time in his letters but in general followed this pattern. The longest openings are found in Galatians 1:1–4 and Romans 1:1–7. These may be explained by the fact that both letters reflect the Judaizing controversy and were written close together. The signature with important details comes in verses 1–6. Paul calls himself "a servant [slave] of Christ Jesus" (1:1, best texts). This was one of his favorite self-designations. Once he was a bondslave to sin; now he is a bondslave to Christ Jesus. The Greek word *doulos* denoted the most servile position in Greek society, but Christian thought raised it to a position of honor. As a slave of "Christ Jesus" (best texts) Paul belonged to Christ and served his interests only. Note that by this time *Christ* had become a personal name, not just an official title. Furthermore, Paul denotes himself as "a called apostle" (*klētos apostolos*). This reflects the Judaizers' denial that he was a true apostle. He was called of God, not appointed by men (Gal. 1:11–2:16). To emphasize that his call is from God rather than from men, Paul adds that he was "separated unto the gospel of God." The verb rendered "separated" means to mark off from a boundary or line (*aphorizō*, note "horizon" in this word). The form here is a perfect passive participle.* The perfect tense expresses completeness. The passive voice means that the separation was done to Paul by another or by God. The idea seems to be that, like Jeremiah (Jer. 1:5), he had been "a called apostle having been separated unto the gospel of God" before his birth. He was separated and still stands separated. In verse 2 Paul sees the gospel as the fulfillment of God's promise through the Old Testament prophets. At the time Paul wrote, the "holy scriptures," of course, were the Old Testament. The New Testament is the flower of which the Old is the bud.

We see in this brief statement the apostle's answer to the Jews who accused him of perverting the divine message. Rather than seeking to destroy God's earlier revelation, he is declaring the gospel which is "of God" as the full, complete revelation of God. Rather than being a renegade Jew, Paul insists that the

---

* References to Greek verb tenses will be made throughout. For those not versed in the Greek language, a brief explanation will prove helpful. Unlike English tenses, in Greek the tense refers primarily to the kind of action expressed, with time being secondary. The *present* tense expresses repeated, continuous, or habitual action. In this tense, an action may be pictured as a line. The *imperfect* tense denotes repeated action in the past but leading up to the present. The *aorist* (*a-oristos*, without limit) tense is called the historical tense. It means that something simply happened in the past. It looks at an action as a point in time, rather than as a line. The *perfect* tense is the tense of completeness. It expresses action which took place in the past and is still true at the time of writing, the inference being that it will continue to be true in the future. The *future* tense denotes an action yet to take place in the future.

Christian gospel is the fulfillment of all that is true in Judaism. Thus in two brief verses he answers the charges of the Judaizers and the non-Christian Jews.

And what is this gospel all about? It is "concerning" God's "Son Jesus Christ our Lord" (v. 3). In the Greek text "his Son" is separated from "Jesus Christ our Lord" by the remainder of the verse. They may be seen as parentheses which are described by the intervening portion. "His Son." And who is he? He is "the one born out of the seed of David according to the flesh, the one appointed or declared [the verb is *horizō*, from which we get our word *horizon*], God's Son in [*en*, in the sphere of] power according to the Spirit of holiness out of resurrection from the dead—Jesus Christ our Lord" (literal). Thus Paul declares both the humanity and deity of Jesus Christ and avows his lordship. Of course, Jesus' resurrection from the dead involves his redemptive death.

Two words call for emphasis at this point. One is the participle rendered "was made" (v. 3). Unlike the verb *to be* which expresses essential being, this verb means "to become" or "to come into being." Note the use of these two verbs in John 1:1 ("was") and John 1:3, 14 ("were made," "was made"). The Word (Christ) *always was*. The created order which did not exist eternally came into being. Also the eternal Christ became something he had not been before—flesh. So in Romans 1:3–4 the eternal Christ became of the seed of David according to the flesh or Jesus of Nazareth, and in his victory over sin and death, he proved his right to lordship (see Phil. 2:6–11). The other word is "dead" (v. 4). It is a plural form and thus denotes that in his resurrection Christ is the "firstfruits" of which the final resurrection is the general harvest.

 Interpreters differ as to the meaning of "the spirit of holiness." Some see "spirit" as Jesus' human spirit in relation to "according to the flesh" (Denney, Robertson, Vincent, Wuest). However, comparing this phrase with Isaiah 63:10 and Psalm 51:11, others see this as "the Holy Spirit." The RSV renders this as "the Spirit of holiness" as does the *New American Standard Bible* (see also Moffatt and the NEB). Moody (p. 164) comments, "The other phrase, *of holiness*, makes clear that it is the Holy Spirit, not the human spirit of Jesus, that is meant, for this is a literal translation of the Hebrew phrase found in Isaiah 63:10 and Psalm 51:11."

With the latter position I agree. Jesus was raised from the dead, not by his human spirit, but by the eternal Spirit of God, who is called both the Spirit of God and the Spirit of Christ (Rom. 8:9). The Holy Spirit is God's Spirit sent forth to do

God's work. He was the conceiving power in Jesus' virgin birth.
The Spirit came upon Jesus in fullness at his baptism. Worthy of
note is the fact that the Gospels do not record Jesus performing
a miracle until after this event. He did his work in the power
of the Spirit. He went to the cross "through the eternal Spirit"
(Heb. 9:14), and God raised him from the dead by the power
of "the Spirit of holiness."

If this view be followed, then in his introduction to his exposition of the gospel Paul includes the triune God (Father, Son,
Spirit). This corresponds to the New Testament teaching that
the triune God was/is involved in the eternal redemptive purpose and work of God.

In verse 5 Paul returns to the idea of his apostleship. "By
[*dia*, through] whom" refers to "Jesus Christ our Lord." Through
Christ Paul received both "grace and apostleship." Paul was
saved by grace, and also by grace he received his apostleship
(Acts 9:3–16). He considered his apostleship as much a gift
from Christ as his salvation, and this apostleship to the Gentiles
(Acts 9:15; Gal. 2:9) was to the end (*eis*, for) that on behalf
of Christ's name Gentiles ("among all nations") should come to
"obedience of faith." Scholars differ as to the meaning of this
phrase. Since "faith" has no definite article in the Greek text, it
probably does not refer to the body of the Christian faith (see
Acts 6:7 where *faith* has the definite article). Here the meaning, as throughout Romans (see 15:18; 16:26), is obedience
which springs from a personal commitment to Christ. This was
the commitment Paul had and which he longs to see among all
believers.

In verse 5 Paul refers to his readers, the Christians in Rome,
as a part of "all the nations" (RSV). He adroitly moves from himself to them. Literally, "among whom are also you called ones
belonging to Jesus Christ." "You" is written out as well as being
present in the verb form; so it is emphatic. The Roman Christians belong to Christ because they have heard and responded
positively to the gospel. This means that they are not "called
ones" to the neglect of others. God calls "in Christ." This phrase
or its equivalent appears ten times in eleven verses in Ephesians
1:3–13. God has elected to save all who are "in Christ" through
faith in him (Eph. 1:13). These readers had believed in him;
so they are "called ones belonging to him."

"To all that be in Rome, beloved of God, called to be saints"
(v. 7). Thus Paul addresses his letter. Belonging to Christ they
are God's "beloved" ones. The Greek text reads "called saints."
They are not called "to be saints"; they *are* "saints" or "holy
ones." The basic idea in this term used to designate believers

is being set apart for God's service. Wuest (p. 18) notes that the words "saint, sanctify, sanctification, holy, hallow" all translate words formed on the same root *hagi.* Here the word is *hagiois.*

The original use of the word *hagi* and its kindred ones expressed not character but relationship. Women used in the sex act by pagan devotees in worship of sex deities were called "holy" since they were set apart for use in service to these sex gods/goddesses. *Holy* took on the moral character of God when it came to be used of him (see Isa. 6:3). Whereas in the Old Testament the word was used more of things (for example, tabernacle, vessels, altar), in the New Testament the greater use regards people. Of course, in the Christian sense "saints" should seek to live in keeping with God's character.

The very moment we are regenerated, we are sanctified, we become "saints," set apart for God's service. We may not always act saintly, but we are saints (see "saints," 1 Cor. 1:2; 2 Cor. 1:1). Thus we do not grow *into* sanctification, but we grow *in the state* of sanctification. Of course, the meaning in the word itself involves service for God.

"Grace to you and peace from God our Father, and the Lord Jesus Christ" (v. 7). This is Paul's greeting in the form of a prayer. The usual Greek greeting was *chaire* (joy to you). The Hebrew greeting was *shalom* (peace). But the Christians used *charis* (grace) and *shalom* (peace). This is found in all Paul's epistles except his letters to Timothy. In those he added "mercy" after "grace" ("mercy" is not in the best texts of Titus 1:4).

The order of these words is significant. One must experience God's *grace* before he can know *peace.* Denney (p. 587) notes that grace and peace are "the source and the sum of all Christian blessings." Wuest (p. 19) says, "The grace which Paul prays will be theirs is grace for daily living in the form of the ministry of the Holy Spirit. The peace is peace of heart, a state of Christian tranquility." This peace is more than happiness. It is serenity of spirit even in the midst of a storm.

The Thanksgiving and Prayer (1:8–12)

With the exception of Galatians, all of Paul's letters follow the usual Greek form of thanksgiving after the signature and salutation. Here the apostle adds the assurance of his constant prayer for his readers.

The "first" in verse 8 is not followed by second, third, and so on. Often Paul uses a similar form, with his onrushing thoughts ignoring such a formality. His thanksgiving is to God through

Jesus Christ "concerning all of you" since their faith or Christian fidelity is proclaimed throughout the "whole world" (the Roman Empire). As in any capital city, events there became known throughout the realm. Though Paul had never been to Rome, he had contact with other Christians who had; so their "faith" was common knowledge among fellow believers everywhere.

Paul calls upon God as his witness that he constantly prays for his readers (v. 9). Prayer is not hindered by dimensions of time and space. Along with many others, Paul had the Roman Christians on his prayer list (1 Thess. 1:2).

Specifically, he prays that somehow, sometime he may be prospered or have a good journey, if it be God's will, to visit Rome (v. 10). He longs to see them for two definite reasons (vv. 11–12): that he may give to them some spiritual gift in order that they may be strengthened in the faith; and that he along with them may be "comforted" or encouraged through one another's faith. Both he and they had heard of each other. What a blessed time they would have together face to face!

The Purpose of Paul (1:13–15)

The King James Version is true to the Greek text when it reads, "Now I would not have you ignorant, brethren" (v. 13). Literally, "Now I do not wish you to be unknowing." This has to do with his previous plans to visit them (Acts 19:21). Many times he had that as his purpose, "but was let [prevented] hitherto" or up to this time. What the hindrance was he does not say. It could be that Satan had thwarted his purpose (1 Thess. 2:18). More likely, it was the demands of the work in the eastern Mediterranean area (Rom. 15:19–22). But now conditions are such that he can fulfill his long-held desire. Though his "fruit" among other Gentiles was great, he wanted to harvest some in Rome also.

Paul labored under the burden of a sense of debtorship (v. 14). The Greek text places the emphasis upon the recipients of the debt: "both to Greeks and Barbarians, both to wise and unwise I am debtor." "Greeks" refers to all non-Jews. The Greeks called all who did not speak their language "barbarians." To them another language sounded like *bar bar;* so they combined these words and added the *os* ending to form *barbaros,* barbarian (see Acts 28:2). "Barbarians" could include Jews and the people of Spain. "Wise and unwise" may read "cultured and uncultured." This is a repetition of the thought in "Greeks . . . Barbarians." The Greeks considered themselves cultured and all others uncultured. Since Rome was permeated by Greek culture and language, the Romans could be included in "Greeks." But regardless of how they were regarded, they were certainly included. In fact, these terms may be seen as referring to the entire human race.

Paul was not a debtor because of anything he had received from them. It was because of what he had received from God in Christ. He was, therefore, under obligation to declare the gospel to others. He singles out Greeks and Barbarians because he was the apostle to the Gentiles. But as we have seen, these terms embrace all people. Certainly Paul was burdened for the Jews (Rom. 9:1–2; 10:1). Would that every Christian shared his sense of debtorship and, like him, sought to pay the debt! If we cannot fully pay it, at least we should try to keep the interest paid up to date. Paul was ready to pay an installment on his debt; to the best of his ability he was "eager" (RSV) to preach the gospel to those living in Rome (v. 15).

The Twofold Nature of the Gospel (1:16–18)

In Romans 1:1–4 Paul analyzed the gospel. Now he returns to that theme. He is ready to preach the gospel in Rome for four reasons. These are seen in the word "for" (gar) in these verses.

First, "For I am not ashamed of the gospel" (v. 16). "Of Christ" is not in the best texts, but the idea is true nevertheless. Actually, Paul used an understatement for effect. Rather than being ashamed of the gospel, he glories in it. Pagan Rome with her pomp and splendor might look with scorn upon such a message. The Jews might stumble over the gospel, and the Greeks might laugh at it (1 Cor. 1:23), but Paul glories in it.

Second, "for it is the power of God unto salvation to every one that believeth; to the Jew first, and also to the Greek" (v. 16). Paul knew this by his own regeneration experience and through his work of proclaiming the gospel. When he faced the wicked city of Corinth, he did so "in fear, and in much trembling" (1 Cor. 2:3), but he had seen what the gospel did there. Now in eager boldness he faces the city which practically worships political and military power. He comes with a power greater than that of Rome. It is God's power, not for destruction and tyranny, but for salvation to all who believe it.

The word for power is dunamis. In the Greek text here it has no definite article; so it is "a power of God" or "God's power," divine power working in the hearts of those who receive the gospel in faith. This power works through the Holy Spirit. Wuest says, "The gospel is the inherent, omnipotent power of

God operating in the salvation of a soul that accepts it" (p. 24).
The resultant "salvation" is not a static experience. It involves
both a *being* and a *becoming*. The New Testament presents it
as regeneration (John 3:7), sanctification (Heb. 2:3), and
glorification (Heb. 9:28). (See Rom. 8:29-30.) Regeneration
is the saving of the soul. Sanctification, simultaneous with regeneration, is the saving of the Christian life. Glorification is
the sum total of glory and reward in heaven, including the
resurrection of the body (Rom. 8:23). These three phases of
salvation are symbolized in Christian baptism (Rom. 6:3-5).
In Ephesians 1:14 "redemption" should read "full-redemption"
or the fullness of salvation. In regeneration we are saved from
the *penalty* of sin. In sanctification we are saved from the
power of sin. In glorification we shall be saved from the *presence* of sin. It is proper, therefore, to say, "I have been saved
(regeneration); I am being saved (sanctification); I will be
saved (glorification)." All this is involved in "salvation" as used
in Romans 1:16.

Third, "for therein is the righteousness of God revealed from
faith to faith: as it is written, The just shall live by faith"
(v. 17). Here and in verse 18 Paul gives the twofold nature of
the gospel. The gospel reveals God's righteousness or the God-
kind-of-righteousness.

In the Bible *righteousness* is used in three ways: that which
God is in his nature; that which he demands in man but which
man cannot achieve within himself; that which God bestows in
Christ. It is in this last sense that *righteousness* is used in Romans. It is not an attribute of God but an activity of God
whereby he picks man up out of the wrong and puts him down
in the right as though he had never been in the wrong (see
Rom. 3:25-26). Of course, God is righteous. He does not arbitrarily ignore or forgive sin, but in his gracious activity through
redemption he declares righteous those who believe in his Son.
It is not of man's doing, as Paul shows in God's revelation of
it "from faith to faith" or, literally, "out of faith unto faith."
It is a matter of faith from beginning to end, made possible by
God's grace. "The just shall live by . . . faith" (Hab. 2:4) is
the only verse from the Old Testament quoted three times in
the New Testament (see also Gal. 3:11; Heb. 10:38).

Worthy of note is the fact that the Greek word for "righteousness" (*dikaiosunē*) belongs to a family of words ending with
ē (*eta*) which means that a thing is not necessarily true but
that one chooses to regard it as true. So a person may not be
righteous within himself, but God in Christ chooses to regard
him as righteous. Thus in the believer God does not see his un-

righteousness but God's righteousness which is in Christ (Rom. 10:3–4). It is not that which man in himself *achieves* but that which in Christ he *receives*.

Fourth, "for the wrath of God is revealed from heaven against all ungodliness and unrighteousness of men, who hold the truth in unrighteousness" (v. 18).

Note that both God's righteousness and wrath are revealed. Though Paul does not repeat "therein" (*en autōi*) in verse 18, it is to be understood from verse 17. So the twofold nature of the gospel is that it expresses both God's righteousness and God's wrath—his righteous act in salvation for the believer and his wrath against the unbeliever.

God's wrath (*orgē*) is not an emotion of God but God's natural, physical, moral, and spiritual law in operation. You do not break God's laws, but rather you are broken by them when you live counter to them. His laws are benevolent. If you live by them, they are a blessing. If you violate them, they take their toll. His laws are intended to do the most good to the most people. For example, the law of gravity is intended to hold a skyscraper as well as people to the earth. If you violate that law by leaping from the skyscraper, God does not repeal the law to save you from a rash act. If he did, the skyscraper and people would be floating about in space. Would not the earth itself explode? It is a law of physics that two solid substances cannot occupy the same space at the same time. If two automobile drivers ignore this fact, the result is a crash producing injury and/or death.

The same reasoning applies to any of the other laws. Certain laws are designed to produce health in the body and the social order, but if violated the result is sickness in both. It is not necessary to multiply examples of this fact for they are everywhere evident. Of course, Paul's primary thought relates to the spiritual order. "The wages of sin is death; but the gift of God is eternal life through Jesus Christ our Lord" (Rom. 6:23). This law is stated comprehensively in Galatians 6:7–8. "Be not deceived; God is not mocked: for whatsoever a man soweth, that shall he also reap" (v. 7). "God is not mocked" may well read, "You cannot turn up your nose at God and get away with it."

Moody (p. 169) rightly relates "ungodliness" and "unrighteousness" to the two sections of the Ten Commandments. The first four deal with man's relation to God (Exod. 20:3–11); the last six deal with man's relation to other men (Exod. 20:12–17). Robertson (p. 328) speaks of ungodliness as "irreligion, want of reverence toward God" and of unrighteousness as "lack of right conduct toward men, injustice." Then he adds, "This follows naturally from irreverence. The basis of ethical conduct rests on the nature of God and our attitude toward him, otherwise the law of the jungle (cf. Nietzsche, 'might makes right')." To "hold [hold down] the truth in unrighteousness" means to ignore God's law which such men know and to live contrary to it. This is true of both Gentile and Jew as Paul presently shows (see Rom. 1:19–3:18).

Before passing on to this analysis, however, it is well to note the nature of God's "wrath." A Greek word frequently used in the New Testament for "wrath" is *thumos*. This word is used of dry grass which burns furiously and rapidly but is soon burnt out. It suggests the sudden eruption of a volcano which subsides quickly. Such wrath of God may be seen in the destruction of Sodom. Fire and brimstone rained down upon the city and soon destroyed it, but Lot and his daughters, though nearby, were safe.

Orgē, the word used here, expresses God's abiding, universal opposition to evil. It is everywhere at all times. John the Baptist used this word when he asked, "Who hath warned you to flee from the wrath to come?" (Matt. 3:7). The picture is that of desert creatures fleeing from a fire which is everywhere. Where is the only safe refuge from such a fire? Only where the fire has already burned. Where can you flee from the *orgē* of God? Only to Calvary where it has already been expressed in fullness against sin as God's Son was made sin for us that through faith in him we might be made God's righteousness in him (see 2 Cor. 5:21).

So the twofold nature of the gospel is that in it are revealed both God's righteous saving act and his abiding, universal opposition toward evil. One cannot preach a whole gospel without declaring both. Indeed, it is against the dark backdrop of God's wrath that his righteousness may be seen in all its glory.

2

The Need for Righteousness

Romans 1:19–2:29

Having set the stage for his discussion of the gospel and its many ramifications, Paul now presents his argument to show why it was necessary for God to save man through the gospel. Intermingled with this theme is also God's wrath against sin.

The need for the revelation of the twofold gospel is seen, not in man's natural growth and success, but in his failure to achieve the righteousness which God demands. In Romans 1:16 Paul said that the gospel is "to the Jew first, and also to the Greek," but in his development of his theme he reverses the order and begins with the Greeks, or pagans. He did this perhaps for two reasons: the Roman church was predominantly Gentile in nature; the question probably was raised then as now as to whether or not God was/is just in his demands upon the Gentiles. We can best understand Romans if we see Paul as answering the questions raised by imaginary opponents in debate.

The Failure of the Gentiles (1:19–32)

As if answering the charge of God's injustice toward Gentiles, Paul shows that they have failed to live according to the knowledge of God which they possess, and all men, whether Gentile or Jew, possess evidence of the existence of God. "Because that which may be known of God is manifest in them; for God hath shewed it unto them" (v. 19). This does not mean that apart from his revelation in Christ all knowledge concerning God is evident to men. The words rendered "that which may be known" may read "the known," "the knowable," or "the knowledge." The knowledge of God's existence is written in every man's heart or conscience (see Rom. 2:14–15). God has made this clear to every man if only he will recognize it.

Furthermore, God has revealed himself in the natural order (v. 20). God himself is invisible or cannot be seen with the natural eye (see John 4:24; Col. 1:15), but the visible things testify to his existence as an infinite, benevolent being. Any

reasoning person can understand this simply by viewing the
beauty and order of the universe, from a lovely flower to the
exact movements of the heavenly bodies (see Job 38–41; Pss.
19, 104; Isa. 40–45). To say that these are products of blind
accident and impersonal force taxes one's credulity far more
than to see behind the creation a Creator. Barclay (p.
18) quotes Tertullian, an ancient early Christian leader:

> "It was not the pen of Moses that initiated the knowledge of the
> Creator. . . . The vast majority of mankind, though they had
> never heard the name of Moses—to say nothing of his book—
> know the God of Moses none the less." "Nature," said he, "is the
> teacher; the soul is the pupil."

The Bible dismisses the so-called atheist with the terse phrase
"The fool [unreasoning person] hath said in his heart, There is
no God" (Ps. 14:1). Note that he said it in his *heart*, the seat
of willing and wishing. In his reason he knows there is a God,
but he wishes there were none to whom he is responsible.

Note that from nature man knows God's "eternal power and
Godhead" (v. 20). "Godhead" should read "Godhood," for Paul
used the Greek word *theiotēs*. In Greek "Godhead" is *theotēs*
(Col. 2:9), the sum-total of deity or its essence. Had Paul used
theotēs here, he would have intended to indicate pantheism,
the idea that everything is God. He carefully avoided this by the
use of *theiotēs* which means that even in the natural order man
can see that God is, that he is benevolent, and that he is worthy
of worship and obedience. For this reason man's rejection of
God is inexcusable. While this is true of both Jew and Gentile,
Paul is thinking primarily of the latter in verses 21–32.

It should be kept in mind that the apostle wrote Romans
while in Corinth, and while in verses 21–23 he deals with paganism in general, in verses 24–32 he describes the very conditions he saw in pagan Corinth. But sadly one may see the
same conditions in our own present world, even in what some
would call Christian America.

Even though pagans knew God through the natural order
and in their consciences, they did not glorify him or give him
thanks as the source of their material blessings. "Know" translates a participle of the verb *to know by experience*. Because
they denied the lesson of experience they became "vain in their
reasonings." "Vain" means futile, fruitless, or without results.
The Greek word for "imaginations" carries the idea of reasonings or thought-deliberations within one's self. Such futile mental reasoning led men into the dry desert of paganism. "Heart"
refers to all one's inner faculties: feeling, intellect, will. "Fool-

ish" is a verbal adjective from the verb meaning to put together. In the negative form, as here, it means being unable to put all together the evidence of God in nature and the conscience. So that darkness settled down upon the inner self. Kant, the German philosopher, is reported as saying that two things never failed to strike awe in his heart: the starry heavens above and the moral law within. The pagan world felt no such awe.

"Professing themselves to be wise [sophoi, sophisticated ones], they became fools" (v. 22). What a scalding condemnation of wisdom devoid of true knowledge! As one has noted, the Greek verb translated "professing" means to make an unfounded or unsupported assertion. The world is filled with such people today. A group of scientists in California cried to high heaven in defeating an effort to place the Genesis account of creation in school textbooks alongside the *theory* of evolution. Evidently they are not as certain of their position as they appear to be. True science is not afraid to subject its positions to information which questions or denies its findings. Evolution is nothing more than *theory,* yet this unfounded assertion is presented as a fact in textbooks and popular magazines.

Paul says that those making professions unsupported by facts "became fools." The verb so translated is *mōrainō* which means to become silly, foolish, insipid, to drivel or play the fool. The noun form is *mōros* which means dull, sluggish, foolish. Our word *moron* comes from it; so such people who appear to be so wise are actually morons in the light of God's truth.

How did they become fools? By changing the glory of the uncorruptible or imperishable God into an image (*eikonos,* icon) made in the likeness of corruptible man, birds, four-footed beasts, and creeping things (v. 23). When men refused to worship God, they made idols designed to express the various facets of God's nature. Only they gave them a base material rather than an exalted spiritual meaning, which explains why the images of gods in the form of beasts and men are so horrible in appearance.

Note the downward trend: men, birds, beasts, and creeping things (snakes and/or insects). Here Paul ran the gamut of pagan worship. The Greeks and Romans worshiped gods in human form. Egypt worshiped the sacred bull Apis, snakes, and bugs such as the scarab or sacred beetle. Serpent-worship was also common in Chaldea.

For many years the champions of evolution insisted that man began by worshiping many gods and gradually some came to worship one god or God. This, of course, denied Genesis 1–2 and Romans 1. But about 1930, working independently, the sciences of anthropology and archaeology concluded that man began by worshiping one God and gradually descended to the worship of many gods. This, of course, coincides with the biblical account.

Beginning with verse 24 Paul says that idolatry led to immorality. As you read this awful description, notice how the sins which abounded in ancient paganism are so prevalent today. If I did not know that Paul was describing the sins of Corinth as typical of paganism, I would think that he was depicting the moral rottenness of modern society. Note also the recurring phrase "God gave them up" (vv. 24, 26, 28). The Greek wording is the same in each case. Robertson says, "The words sound to us like clods on the coffin as God leaves men to work their own wicked will" (p. 330).

Someone called Paul a "wherefore" preacher. On the basis of evidence already presented, he draws a conclusion or shows how what he has said develops. In this case it was to deteriorate into rottenness of the worst sort.

In verses 24–25 the apostle makes a general statement and then follows it with specifics in succeeding verses. "Wherefore God gave them up." There comes a time when with rebellious people, as one would do with a rebellious horse, God removes the bridle to permit his violated moral laws to work out to their own end. That he does not do this arbitrarily is evident in the Greek text: "Wherefore God gave them up [handed them over] in the sphere of the evil desires [lusts] of their hearts unto uncleanness of the dishonoring of their bodies among themselves" (literal).

Since God made man a free moral agent, he does not coerce him against his own will. Man is free to choose but is responsible for his choices. This is seen in Genesis 1–3 which Moody sees as the root of Romans 1:18–22. Adam chose to obey the serpent (devil) rather than God, and from that point on we see the terrible fruits of such a choice.

All this stems from men changing the truth of God into a lie. "Changed" really means "exchanged" as in trade. Adam swapped God's truth for the devil's lie (Gen. 2:16–17; 3:1–6). He worshiped "the creature [serpent] more than the Creator" (v. 25). This is the essence of idolatry. It does not mean that Adam's sin was sexual in nature, merely that he chose to follow the devil rather than God. However, pagan idolatry centers in the sensual and sexual, as Paul proceeds to show. The remainder of this chapter shows its fruit in immorality (vv. 24–27) and spiritual wickedness (vv. 28–32).

Thus God gave them up "unto vile affections," literally, "passions of dishonor." "Passions" (*pathē*, note "pathos") meant feelings good or bad, but in the New Testament this Greek word is always used in the bad sense (see 1 Thess. 4:5; Col. 3:5). This resulted in every kind of sex perversion. The natural was "exchanged" for perverted sex activity. Even females lusted after each other, which is contrary to nature (lesbians). Both males and females became homosexual rather than heterosexual (v. 27). The words used here mean "females" and "males" rather than the usual terms which are translated "women" and "men." "Unseemly" means "against nature." Even animals do not sink so low!

Homosexuality is no new practice (see 1 Cor. 6:9); it was common in the ancient pagan world. Most of the early Caesars were homosexual. Suetonius describes Julius Caesar as "every woman's man and every man's woman." The present "gay generation" is but a modern counterpart of ancient paganism. Indeed, this may be said of all illicit sexual behavior. That which God gave as one of the most beautiful and meaningful parts of marriage, paganism ancient and modern has degraded into the most sordid of sins in its illicit and unnatural expression. Efforts are being made today to bring homosexuality under the respectable cloak of religion. It is now and has always been under a religious cloak, but the religion was/is paganism. Efforts to bring it or any other illicit sexual behavior into the Christian orbit is little less than blasphemy itself. In fact, we may even with good reason delete the words "little less than." Without exception the Bible condemns homosexuality and all other illicit sex practices. Abuse of sex saps the strength and tears the moral fiber of a nation. It has been one of the harbingers of the fall of nations throughout the recorded history of man.

Verse 28 refers to intellectual idolatry, the most vicious of all. The words "did . . . like" render a verb for testing as of coins. Men tested God and did not find him to their liking. His moral character and demands did not satisfy the standard of the kind of God they wanted; so they rejected him. They did not like "to have God in full-knowledge." That they had a faint memory of him is seen in the objects of worship they chose. Out of this dim memory they made caricatures of God. They did not acknowledge the true God but made gods in keeping with their baser natures. They made their minds superior to God's mind in determining what for them was good and right. This is the original "situation ethics" and "new morality." They were then and are now subterfuges to allow men to give unbridled lusts a means of expression in the name of religion. Men made in God's image made gods in their own image. To their own hurt they rejected the moral basis of the universe as later expressed in the Ten Commandments. Thus they did those things which are not "convenient," fitting or proper (v. 28).

For God gave them up "to a reprobate mind" (v. 28), or a mind incapable of reason and drawing proper conclusions. Denney sums up the whole in a vivid statement:

> As they did not think fit, after trial made (*edokimasan*), to keep God in their knowledge, God gave them up to a mind which cannot stand trial (*adokimon*). The one thing answers to the other. Virtually, they pronounced the true God *adokimos*, and would have none of Him; and He in turn gave them up to a *nous adokimos*, a mind which is no mind and cannot discharge the functions of one, a mind in which the Divine distinctions of right and wrong are confused and lost, so that God's condemnation cannot but fall on it at last. *Nous* is not only reason, but conscience; when this is perverted, as in the people of whom Paul speaks, or in the Caananites, who did their abominations *unto their Gods* [gods], the last deep evil has been reached (p. 594).

It is no wonder that God dropped/drops the last "clod" on their coffin!

Verses 29–32 list some of the pagan sins which "are not convenient." It should be noted that these fruits of intellectual idolatry refer largely to sins of the spirit. These, as well as all sins, are both anti-God and antisocial. The Greek word translated "being filled" is a perfect participle of completeness. Those who did not glorify God are filled to the brim and overflowing in such sins. "Unrighteousness" summarizes them all, and a colon might well be placed after it, thus letting the other twenty-one sins, including verse 32, flow from it. "Fornication" does not appear in the best texts. It is hardly necessary to deal with these sins individually. Reference to any good modern translation will express them in modern thought (see RSV, TEV), but note should be taken of verse 32 which is the climax of "unrighteousness." Even though pagans have full knowledge of God's condemnation of such sins and know that those practicing them are worthy of death, they not only have the habit of doing them but delight in others who have the habit of practicing them. This suggests that they not only enjoy common pleasures with sinners but enjoy encouraging others to do them. This is plumbing the depths of iniquity. It is total defiance of God and complete disregard for the moral and spiritual good of others. Such is God's judgment upon paganism in all ages of history—today as in the past.

The Failure of the Jews (2:1-24)

Paul now turns to the Jews and their failure with respect to keeping God's written law. Intermingled with God's judgment upon disobedient Jews is his judgment upon rebellious Gentiles or pagans (vv. 8–16; see also 3:9–20). The apostle's primary purpose in this section is to show that Jews as well as pagans need the God-kind-of-righteousness.

Paul continues his debate with imaginary opponents or questioners (see "O man," v. 1). In this case the questioner is a Jew as representative of all Jews. Certainly he agrees with Paul's terrible description of the sins of paganism. After all, what would one expect of Gentile dogs? Were they not, indeed, "fuel for the fires of hell," as one rabbi stated it? However, the Jew is quite another matter. Is he not God's chosen, and does he not, therefore, bear a special relation to God? Judgment upon pagans? Yes! But not upon Jews. Indeed, they themselves sit in judgment against the pagans.

But Paul answers his Jewish questioner by beginning with "therefore" (*dio*), the same word translated "wherefore" in 1:24. This refers here to the Jewish questioner's assent to Paul's condemnation of the pagans. Since the Jew, like the pagan, does not live up to the knowledge he has of God's will, his very assent to the judgment upon the pagans sits in judgment upon him. In fact, his sin is even greater because it is against a greater light from God. Thus the Jew is also "inexcusable" (v. 1), the same basic word used of pagans in 1:20. The English word *apology* in the sense of a defense comes from this root. So the Jew also has no defense before God for his conduct. He is in the same boat with the pagan world.

"Whosoever thou art that judgest" reads literally "every single one who is judging" the pagans. "Judging" means to pick out or separate between two things. Here the selection is between right and wrong, and the Jew sees the pagan as in the wrong. However, Paul says that in judging the pagans, the Jew condemns himself. "Condemnest" is the translation of a Greek verb meaning to judge down, so to condemn. In other words, the one doing the judging practices the same things.

Sexual immorality was not as prevalent among Jews as among pagans, but it was a besetting sin to them. The Old Testament tells the sad story of the Israelites' worshiping the golden calf and the gods of the Canaanites, both of which involved sexual immorality. Jews were certainly filled with the social and spiritual sins listed in 1:29–32, and "we [Jews] know" that God judges according to the truth (v. 2). His judgment squares with the facts in the case (Denney, p. 595). God does not have *favorites* in his courtroom. The word *oida* is translated "know" and means full, perceptive knowledge. It is a soul conviction as to God's method of judgment.

In verse 3 Paul repeats "O man, the one judging" as once again he singles out his Jewish questioner. Does the Jew think that in practicing the same sins as the pagans he "may flee from the judgment of God"? This question and the one in verse 4 lays bare what Moody (p. 173) calls "the very nerve of Judaism." Not only will the Jew not escape God's judgment, he also misinterprets God's rich goodness, forbearance, and long-suffering. "Despisest" means to think down upon something. Rather than these things being God's ignoring the Jews' sins or making Jews his favorites, they are designed to lead them to "repentance." *Repentance* means a turning about of mind (one's inner self), a complete change of heart, will, and the direction of one's life. The Jews were going away from God, but God longs for them to return to him in loving, willing repentance and faith. Repentance and faith are inseparable graces. If you truly repent of sin, you will trust in Christ for salvation.

However, instead of repenting, the Jews continued to live in smug complacency, thinking that they were God's favored people. But in their hardness and nonrepentance of heart, they were simply storing up a treasure unto themselves which consisted of "wrath [*orgē*, see 1:18] in the day of wrath and revelation [unveiling] of God's righteous judgment" (v. 5). The compound Greek word *dikaiokrisias* is translated "righteous judgment." It will be a judgment in accord with all the facts. "Wrath" here is eschatological in nature. In 1:18 it relates to anywhere, any time, but "in the day of wrath" shows that here Paul is thinking of the final judgment. This wrath will be all the greater because it is stored up. It is like water held back by a dam until one day the dam breaks, and the water rushes out in a destructive flood (see 2:8). Judgment then will not be simply for the sin itself but for its fruit accumulated by its wicked influence in the lives of others through the ages. This is why the final judgment for every person is delayed until the end of the age. A righteous judgment cannot be rendered until all the evidence is in.

Then God "will render to every man according to his deeds" (v. 6). "Render" is the translation of a verb meaning "to pay back." Barclay translates this passage, "Settle accounts with each man according to his deeds" (p. 40). "Deeds" may be translated "works" (RSV). Note that whereas in 2:2 Paul speaks of judgment "according to truth," here he speaks of it "according to works." Three things call for notice.

First, the Jews thought of themselves as God's "chosen people." They forgot that they were chosen for responsibility (Exod. 19:1–6), and they thought of privilege or that they were God's favorites. They believed their judgment, if any, would be on a different basis than that for Gentiles. Paul reminds them that "each man" must stand in judgment, not as a Jew or as a Gentile or as a nation, but as one person. This truth is evident even from their Scriptures, for here Paul quotes Proverbs 24:12. Furthermore, he repeats the same idea in 2 Corinthians 5:12.

Second, the account will be settled "according to his works." This should not be construed to mean that one's soul salvation is in any way related to works. In Ephesians 2:8–10 Paul clearly denies this idea (see Rom. 4; Gal.). However, the same passage says that while we are not saved by works, we are saved "unto good works." Good works are the fruit, not the root, of regeneration, but Paul agrees with James 2:14–26 that a saving faith will be demonstrated in good works.

In the sense of salvation, good works may be seen as related to sanctification or the saving of the Christian life. In 1 Corinthians 3:11–15 Paul shows that one may have a saved soul but a lost Christian life.

Third, the idea of settling accounts or paying back involves degrees of reward in heaven and punishment in hell. The final judgment will not *decide* but will *declare* whether or not one's soul is saved. That will be determined the moment one dies or at the Lord's return if one is living at that time. This thought of degrees is inherent in 2 Corinthians 5:10, but degrees of reward (glorification) and punishment will be determined by how one utilizes his opportunities in this life (see Luke 12:47–48; 19:12–26). Note that "the dead [lost and saved] were judged out of those things which were written in the books, according to their works" (Rev. 20:12).

An analysis of Romans 2:7–10 shows that Paul is thinking of good works as evidence of salvation and evil works as evidence of the lack of it, but as Moody says, "A judgment on the basis of works is not the same as justification by works" (p. 174).

Verse 7 deals with the saved: "To the ones on the one hand who by patience [patient endurance] of a good work are seeking glory and honor and incorruptibility, life eternal" (literal). "Patience" is the quality of an athlete or soldier who can take all his opponent throws at him yet possess reserve strength with which to countercharge to victory. To live a full Christian life involves struggle (see Rom. 7), but the reward is worth it both here and hereafter. "Life eternal" is that quality of life one has here and which abides in eternity.

Verses 8–9 treat the unsaved. "But to the ones on the other

hand who are factious and obey not the truth, but obey unrighteousness, wrath [*orgē*], and burning rage [*thumos*]. Tribulation
and anguish upon every soul of man, the one fully working evil,
of the Jew first and also of the Greek" (literal). Note the combination of *orgē* and *thumos* (see 1:18). In the final judgment
God's abiding, universal opposition to evil bursts out into a
burning fire. These words are used in combination in Revelation, with *thumos* being used singly more often than *orgē*.

Verse 10 repeats the general idea of verse 7. Note that both
of these pictures end with "Jew first" and "also Greek." There is
no difference before God whether it involves reward or punishment. "For there is not with God a respect of persons" (v. 10,
literal). In translating this well-known phrase, Wuest uses the'
word *partiality*, and Barclay uses *favouritism*. The Greek word
means to take note of the face, to judge by the face (see Acts
10:34; Gal. 2:6; Eph. 6:9). Racial distinctions appear in the
face more than in any other part of the body. So God judges
Jew and Gentile alike.

In Romans 2:5 Paul spoke of the "righteous judgment of
God." Now in verses 12–16 he shows how this righteous judgment applies to Gentiles (pagans) and Jews, and in that order.
In essence, Paul says that God will judge each according to the
light of God's revelation which he possesses. These verses answer not only Paul's imaginary Jewish questioner but also those
who question God's condemnation of the heathen who do not
have the Bible or who have never heard the gospel or the name
of Jesus.

In verses 12–13 Paul states a general principle involving both
Gentiles and Jews. Gentiles who sin "without law shall perish
without law." Jews who sin "in the sphere of law, through law
shall be judged" (v. 12, literal).

In the Greek, there is no definite article with *law* throughout
this verse. Obviously here the apostle has in mind the Mosaic law, and the absence of the definite article should not be
stressed. At times the article is to be understood, especially when
the emphasis is upon the concept of law rather than upon the
historical giving of the law of Moses. However, at times in this
discussion the absence of the article is significant, especially
when *law* is compared to *the law* (see v. 14). The context must
decide in each case. Treating verse 12 Wuest quotes Vincent:
"Both law in the abstract and the Mosaic law. The principle laid
down in general, though apparently viewed with special reference to the law of Moses" (p. 43).

Thus Gentiles who do not possess the Mosaic law will be
judged, not by it, but by the light of God's law which is revealed

in nature (1:19–20) and in their hearts (2:15). Jews who have the more complete revelation of God in their Scriptures will be judged by them. However, the absence of the definite article in all these references to *law* makes it possible to expand the meaning to include any system of legalism. The focal point with regard to the Jews, however, is the Mosaic law. "Perish" is the opposite of "eternal life" in verse 7. Both "perish" and "judged" in this context carry the meaning of condemnation (see John 3:16–18).

The principle of judgment is set forth in verse 13. Not those who merely hear law are just before God, but "the ones doing law shall be justified." The Greek word for "hearers" connotes, not simply the act of hearing, but those who are constant hearers and thus are educated in the law. Here Paul is simply repeating the idea found in Leviticus 18:5. *Keeping* the statutes is *doing* them. Those who do them "shall live in them." In Romans 2:13 the apostle applies this principle to both Jews and Gentiles (see James 1:22). *Hearing* may be done with no proper response given to what one knows. *Doing* involves faith and commitment to which God responds in his righteous act of salvation with respect to both Jew and Gentile. Implied is the idea of a greater condemnation for the Jew because he has the greater revelation of God's law.

But what about the Gentile and law? Paul answers this question in verses 14–15. "For when Gentiles, the ones not having law, by nature do habitually the things of the law, these not having law are a law to themselves" (v. 14, literal). Paul assumes a case in which Gentiles do not have a written law such as the Jews have but who by nature keep on doing the things written in "the law," or Mosaic law, and therefore make these things their own law. Note the definite article here.

Paul's use of the Mosaic law refers to the Ten Commandments. They are not true because they are in the Bible; they are in the Bible because they are eternally true and consist of the moral basis of the universe. In one form or another, though the first four may be violated by pagans, certain of the other six, other than the seventh in the worship of sex deities, are moral and legal guides even among those who never heard of Moses and the Ten Commandments. Thus these became a law unto themselves. Many non-Judeo-Christian societies have strong moral scruples against illicit sex. For instance, while rape is one of the most prevalent crimes in America, I am told by missionaries that it is rare in Japan.

This observance by pagans of laws contained in the Decalogue Paul explains by saying that this shows that "the work of the

law" (Mosaic law) is "written in their hearts" (v. 15). So
whether written in stone, on parchment, or in the heart, it is
God's law nevertheless. This law is not as obvious in pagan
hearts, but pagans are responsible for the law they have within
their moral consciousness. This is what the Greeks called "un-
written law." Paul uses "hearts" in the sense of the totality of
the inner person.

Added to this is the work of the conscience which gives a
joint-witness with the moral consciousness as to right and
wrong. The Greek word translated "conscience" means co-
knowledge-alongside the moral consciousness. The conscience
says, "Do right." The moral consciousness says what is right.
The conscience devoid of God's moral judgment may not always
be right. But in those things that are right, the conscience
through reasonings either accuses or excuses one's deeds.

To comprehend verse 16 you must see verses 13–15 as a
parenthetical statement. In verse 16 Paul completes the thought
in verse 12. Whether one is without the Mosaic code or has it,
since God is no respecter of persons, both Jew and Gentile "shall
be judged by the law [which he has] . . . in the day God judges
the secrets [hidden things] of men according to my gospel
through Christ Jesus" (vv. 12, 16, literal). "My gospel" is the
one Paul preaches. It, of course, is God's gospel (1:1), but Paul
can speak of it as his in contrast to those teachings which are
contrary to it (see Judaizers; see also 1 Cor. 15:1–4; Gal.
1:6–9). "The day" refers to the final judgment. Both pagan and
Jew will be judged according to the light he has. The greater
the light of God's revelation, the greater the responsibility and
condemnation for falling short of it. We can trust God to render a "righteous judgment" (2:5).

At this point it will be well to raise a question. Both Jew and
pagan will be condemned at the judgment for failure to live up
to the law of God which he has. Can a person be saved by keeping this law? The answer must be in the affirmative (see Lev.
18:5; Deut. 5:32–33; 6:25; Matt. 19:16–17; Rom. 2:6–7, 10).
However, there is one reservation. To do this one must keep all
of this law all the time. James 2:10–11 shows that to break one
law is to be guilty of all, or that one is as guilty as if he had
broken all. No man does as well as he knows; thus he is lost.
Robertson says, "Jesus alone lived a sinless life. For one to be
saved without Christ he must also live a sinless life" (p. 337).
It is not that man *could* not be saved by keeping law but that he
would not. Thus Paul is right when he says, "Therefore out of
works of law shall not be justified any flesh in his sight" (Rom.
3:20, literal). This is why the God-kind-of-righteousness is nec-

essary. This is why salvation must be by grace through faith in
Jesus Christ.

Having dealt with the matter of Gentiles and law, Paul now
turns to the Jews and their relation to the law (vv. 17–24). He
begins by showing the Jews' feeling of superiority over Gentiles
(vv. 17–20). Rather than the word "behold" at the beginning of
verse 17, the best texts have the particle (*ei*) which introduces
a condition assumed as being true, so "assuming you may be
called a Jew." "You" is emphatic in contrast to "Gentiles" (v. 14).
Then follow certain Jewish attitudes which grow out of this fact.
These have to do with the proper functions of Israel as God's
priest-nation (Exod. 19:5–6) to pagan peoples. However, the
Jews made them a matter of pride, thus alienating the very
people to whom they were to minister.

"Restest" (v. 17) means to lean upon, to refresh oneself back
upon. Paul saw the Jews as resting in the law but making it a
mechanical rather than a spiritual experience. They gloried in
God but made God their own private possession. They claimed
that they alone knew God's will. They proved by testing "the
things that differ," the result being that they approved the ex-
cellent things. This came by being instructed out of "the law."
The verb translated "instructed" means to be taught as though
learning a catechism. They knew the letter but not the spirit of
the law. They were confident that they themselves were destined
to be a guide to the blind, a light to those in darkness, an in-
structor (child-leader, corrector) of the foolish, a teacher of
infants. The Jews had the form (rough sketch) of knowledge
and truth in the sphere of the law (Mosaic law). All these
terms (blind, those in darkness, foolish, infants) the Jews applied to Gentiles, not in compassion, but in scorn. Robertson
says, "This is Paul's picture of the Jew as he sees himself drawn
with consummate skill and subtle irony" (p. 339).

And then Paul began to *meddle* as he asked his imaginary
Jewish questioner how his conduct squared with his position.
A teacher of the law, yes, but was he a doer of it? Did he practice what he preached? These questions the apostle raises in
verses 21–24. As a person teaching another, do you teach yourself? "Another" here means another of a different kind, so a
Gentile. The one proclaiming "Do not steal," do you steal? The
one saying not to commit adultery, do you commit adultery?
The one abhorring idols, do you rob temples? The Greek word
translated "commit sacrilege" (v. 22) is formed out of the word
for "temple" and the verb "to rob." Such a charge was sometimes
made against Jews (see Acts 19:37), although the practice was
"expressly forbidden the Jews (Josephus, *Antiquities* IV, 8, 10).

Paul refers to the crime of robbing idol temples in spite of the defilement of contact with idolatry" (Robertson, p. 339).

Paul plunges his mental sword into the heart of the matter in verses 23–24. "You who boast in the sphere of law, through the transgression [stepping aside] of the law [Mosaic law] do you not dishonor God?" The form of this question invites an affirmative answer. "For the name of God through you is blasphemed [spoken insultingly against] among the Gentiles, as it has been and stands written" (v. 24). "As it is written" refers to Isaiah 52:5.

The Jews reverenced God's name. They would not even pronounce the Tetragrammaton, the four letters YHWH from which the word *Jehovah* is formed. This was the special name for the true God of Israel. Yet the Jews' conduct belied the name of their God. Gentiles judged their God through what they saw in Jewish lives, hence, their blasphemy against God's name. The world always judges the Lord by what it sees in his people.

The True Circumcision (2:25–29)

Having shown that both Gentiles and Jews are responsible to God on the basis of law, Paul now turns to the matter of circumcision which was a basic element in the Jewish religion. Originally it was the sign of the covenant of promises made to Abraham and his seed (see Gen. 17:10–14). By the first century it had taken on tremendous religious value. Since a circumcised person was seen as a child of Abraham, circumcision was regarded as a guarantee against Gehenna, the place of eternal punishment. Before a Jew could be thrown into Gehenna, his sign of circumcision would have to be removed, so the Jews believed. But Paul, while not abrogating the rite of circumcision, shows that more is involved.

There is value in circumcision only to one who makes a habit of practicing the law (v. 25). If one breaks the law, his circumcision becomes uncircumcision. But a Jew is no better than a Gentile. This statement was religious dynamite then! Galatians was written within the context of the Judaizer controversy. Certain Christian Jews sought to force circumcision and the keeping of the Mosaic law upon Gentiles as prerequisites of salvation after believing in Christ (see Gal. 2:1–21; 5:1–12; 6:15; see also Acts 15). Paul in a more reasoned manner here turns the issue around. Rather than Gentiles becoming Jews, Jews who do not keep the law are no better than Gentiles (see Acts 15:10–11).

Furthermore, if the "uncircumcision" (Gentiles) keep the

righteousness of the law, "shall not his uncircumcision be counted [entered into God's accounts] as circumcision?" (v. 26). God will regard him the same as he does the Jew who keeps the law. Both then must be saved by grace through faith in Christ. Moody says, "The believing Gentile is an Abraham before circumcision and the law (cf. Rom. 4). God accepts all who have faith" (p. 178). Verse 27 simply means that the Gentile who by nature fulfills the law judges the Jew who is a law-breaker so that they are then on even terms before God. Paul explains this in verses 28–29.

The true Jew or child of Abraham is not one who simply bears the outward sign of circumcision but one who is inwardly circumcised in heart—in the Holy Spirit, not merely in the letter of the law. This kind of Jew has praise from God, not simply from men. "Praise" (v. 29) may refer to the root meaning of "Jew." Jews derived their name from "Judah." In the Old Testament this name is associated with the Hebrew verb *yadah,* meaning "praise" (Gen. 29:35; 49:8).

Barclay sums it up in telling words.

> The sense of the passage is that God's promises are not to people of a certain race and to people who bear a certain mark on their bodies. They are to people who live a certain kind of life irrespective of their race. To be a real Jew is not a matter of pedigree but of character; and often the man who is not racially a Jew may be a better Jew than the man who is (p. 47).

Verses 25–29 throw light upon Paul's discussion of Jew and Gentile in Romans 9–11.

Thus up to this point Paul has shown by comparison that God truly is no respecter of persons. Though the Jew enjoys certain advantages over the Gentile (for example, the law), Jew and Gentile actually stand on equal footing before God. Each needs a Savior. This thought the apostle develops in Romans 3.

3

The Provision for Righteousness

Romans 3:1–31

Men could not or would not achieve the righteousness which God demands in them. Therefore, either man must be left in a hopeless state, or else God in mercy and grace must provide the means whereby he could bestow righteousness upon man in keeping with God's holy, righteous nature. As holy and righteous he could not condone or ignore sin, but as gracious love neither could he fail to provide man the opportunity to receive as a gift this righteousness, the state of being justified before God. Loving forgiveness was in God's heart before sin was in man's heart. In this light we can understand Jesus Christ as the Lamb slain from the foundation of the world (Heb. 9:26). The redemptive work in eternity must be wrought out in the arena of history. This was done in the life, atoning death, and bodily resurrection of God's Son (see Heb. 10:5–13). It was thus that God took the initiative in saving men (see John 6:40, 44). This initiative is seen in Romans 3 as Paul shows that God in Christ has made provision whereby all men, Jew and Gentile, may be made God's righteousness in Christ.

The Advantage of the Jews (3:1–8)

The chapter break does not constitute a break in Paul's thought, but it does introduce a new phase of his dealing with Jew and Gentile in God's saving purpose. He has shown that both need salvation. Now he proceeds to show how God has condemned sin in both but also has provided a means of salvation for all men.

"What advantage then hath the Jew? or what profit is there of circumcision?" (v. 1). Here the apostle uses a Hebrew parallelism, stating the same idea in two ways. "Advantage" (*perisson*, overflow) may read "overplus." Is the Jew in a better position to be saved than is the Gentile?

Paul says yes, "much every way," or from all angles from which the matter is viewed (v. 2). Then he starts to enumerate the angles. "Chiefly" in verse 2 means "first," but in typical

Pauline fashion, he mentions only one advantage (see Rom. 1:8; 1 Cor. 11:18). Since he did not follow with "second" or "third," "chiefly" is a good translation. The Revised Standard Version reads, "To begin with," but Paul still lists only one angle. However, as Moody (p. 179) points out, Paul returns to this thought in Romans 9:1–5. But for the moment Paul is showing that the Jew as well as the Gentile needs the God-kind-of righteousness.

The advantage cited here is that the Jews have been entrusted with "the oracles of God." "Oracles" is translated from the Greek *logia* which is related to *logos* or "word," so "the word of God." Denney (p. 603) sees this as "the contents of revelation, having God as their author." This means that the Jew had the fuller revelation (compared to Gentiles) of God's will and also the messianic hope. This "advantage," then, was actually a greater obligation to live as God wills.

As if in a dialogue with his imaginary Jewish questioner, Paul raises certain questions and proceeds to answer them (vv. 3–8). Even though the Jews were the custodians of God's oracles, some, in fact many, "did not believe" (v. 3). This verb may mean unbelief or it may connote unfaithfulness. The two ideas are intermingled. Because they did not believe God's word, the Jews were unfaithful to him and their covenant relationship. But does this mean that God's faithfulness to his covenant shall be made "without effect"? The idea here is that of operation rather than effect, hence "inefficient."

Since this is spoken within the context of the Jew's claim to a special relation to God (2:17–29), Paul's statement should be related to the Mosaic covenant at Sinai (Exod. 19:1–6). Note "if" and "then" in Exodus 19:5. It was a conditional covenant. God is not bound by the "then" except as Israel fulfills the "if." Paul's words in Romans 2:25–29 might lead the Jews to accuse him of saying that God is unfaithful if he does not regard them above the Gentiles. However, God stands ready to fulfill his promise to Israel whenever she obeys his voice and keeps his commandments. His promise still stands. Thus unfaithfulness is on the part of the Jews, not on God's part. They rejected the covenant and God's prophets and killed his Son (see Matt. 21:33–45). In that sense, therefore, they were no different from the Gentiles who rejected God's law in nature and their hearts, received no prophets, and participated in the crucifixion of Jesus.

To the idea that he might regard God as unfaithful, Paul replies with his strong "God forbid" (v. 4). Literally, "let it [such a thought] not come into being." Or as we would say, "Perish the thought!" Let God be found true even if every single man is a liar! Truth is one of the moral attributes of God. You might as well say that he is not holy, righteous, or love, as to say that he is not true. To support his statement Paul quotes Psalm 51:4, David's great penitential psalm. God's judgment upon the Jews is justified. Suggested also is that if they repented as did David, God is eager and ready to forgive and restore (see Ps. 32). Note that in the King James Version (see also RSV) "art judged" is in the passive voice, putting God on trial. In Greek the voice may be either passive or middle.* Obviously the latter is appropriate here: "in the entering upon trial as to thee" (Robertson); "when you enter upon judgment" with man (Moody). Thus Romans 3:4 agrees with Psalm 51. In such a trial God will always win or be found true.

In verse 5 Paul raises another question, and answers it with three more questions (vv. 5–7). "But if our [Jews'] unrighteousness commend the righteousness of God, what shall we say?" Paul actually uses himself as an example (v. 7) in order to assuage the wrath of offended Jews, or he refers to himself since Jews were accusing him of false teaching as to God's faithfulness and righteousness (see v. 8). "Is God unrighteous, the one bringing to bear the [his] wrath?" The question calls for a negative reply.

Then Paul adds parenthetically, "I speak as a man." This does not mean that he disclaims divine inspiration. Rather he means that his method of arguing the matter is that used by Stoic philosophers and even Jewish rabbis. It is called a *diatribe*. He poses a question, and then replies with other questions. It is as though he were debating with Jews in a synagogue.

To the question in verse 5 Paul replies with his exclamation "God forbid!" (see v. 4). For if that be true, how does God judge the world (v. 6)? He certainly does not judge it in unrighteousness (see 2:5). If the truth of God has "more abounded" or overflowed through Paul's lie, why then is he judged as a sinner (v. 7)? Paul's former friends in Judaism regarded him as a renegade and held that his sufferings for the gospel were indeed a judgment from God. So their concept did not square with the facts if it were true that Paul was preaching a lie.

In verse 8 the apostle notes the slanderous claim made by some that his gospel of grace encourages people to sin. "Let us

---

* The middle voice in Greek has no direct English equivalent. Basically it is a use of the verb that describes the subject as participating in the results of the action. The active voice emphasizes the action, the middle voice emphasizes the agent, while the passive voice shows the subject as *receiving* the action.

do evil in order that there may come the good" (literal). Paul
puts this in the form of another question. Upon those making
this charge, says Paul, judgment is justified. Of course, Paul
had not said this (he deals with this charge more at length in
chapter 6), but some were justifying their sinful living on this
basis. The apostle emphatically denies that such action is justified on the basis of God's gracious salvation.

The *advantage* of the Jew, therefore, entails a liability upon
those Jews who are unfaithful to their covenant with God. Any
charge which they make against God's salvation by grace
through faith is refuted by cold logic, to say nothing about the
legal demands for righteousness. With this Paul moves on to
declare once again the equal need for salvation on the part of
both Jew and Gentile.

The Condemnation of Jews and Gentiles (3:9–20)

Even though the Jews enjoy certain advantages over the
Gentiles, outside of Christ they both stand condemned before
God. The following verses are second only to Paul's recitation
of the sins of pagans in severity (see 1:19–32).

Paul shifts from Jews alone to both Jews and Gentiles with
his typical "What then?" which Denney (p. 605) paraphrases,
"How, then, are we to understand the situation?" The meaning
of the following question "Are we better than they?" is disputed. Its interpretation ranges all the way from "Do we excell
Gentiles?" to "Are we excelled by Gentiles?" to "Are we in worse
case than the Gentiles?" A rare Greek verb is used in this con-
struction which accounts for these differing opinions; however,
the context (see vv. 1–2) seems to call for the first phraseology;
so the King James Version is not bad here. The Revised Standard Version reads, "Are we Jews any better off?"

Paul answers his own question with a terse "Not at all!"
(*ou pantōs*). "For we have before proved both Jews and Gentiles,
that they are all under sin" (v. 9). The verb translated "before
proved" means to make a prior accusation. *Proved* is a little
strong. Wuest quotes Vincent: "The reference is not to logical
proof, but to forensic accusation" (p. 55). Paul, however, has
made a strong case against both (see 1:19–32; 2:1–29). Even
though the Jew has certain advantages, his behavior shows that
he has failed to utilize them. Both the Jew and the Gentile stand
before the bar of God's judgment charged equally with "sin."
Notice that here for the first time in the epistle Paul uses the
singular of *sin*. Heretofore he has talked about sinful acts.
Here he uses the idea of the sin principle or the power of evil

which dominates the lives of unredeemed men. This fact plays a great part in subsequent discussions in Romans (see 5:12, 21; 6:6-7, 12, 14 for some examples of this).

Verses 10-18 read like a bill of particular charges a lawyer would use in court to prove his case against a defendant. These are formed by the use of portions of certain psalms to which is added one quotation from Isaiah. Note "As it is written" (v. 10). Moody lists Psalms 14:1-3; 5:10; 140:4; 10:7; 36:2; and Isaiah 59:7-8 and notes that behind these Scriptures are the two tables of the law summarized in a positive way as love for God and love for man (p. 181; see the margin of Nestle's Greek Testament—*Novum Testamentum Graece*). These verses may be grouped so as to see Paul speaking as a philosopher (vv. 10-14), a physician (vv. 13-14), and as a historian (vv. 15-18). I propose to treat them in this manner.

First, Paul speaks as a philosopher. "There is none righteous, no, not one: There is none that understandeth, there is none that seeketh after God. They are all gone out of the way, they are together become unprofitable; there is none that doeth good, no, not one" (vv. 10-12).

After searching, the conclusion is that there is not a righteous person, not even one. The Lord promised to save Sodom if ten righteous people could be found there (Gen. 18:23-32). Ten were not found, so God's judgment fell upon the city. God promised to spare Jerusalem "if ye can find a man, if there be any that executeth judgment [justice], that seeketh the truth; and I will pardon it" (Jer. 5:1). Not one was found; so Jerusalem fell to the Babylonians. So why should not God's judgment fall upon the human race since there is not a righteous one, not even one? The remainder of these verses enlarge upon this statement.

No one comprehends or has understanding of the deep things of life. No one with determination really searches for God (v. 11). All have *leaned out,* or turned aside, from the right way. Together they are "unprofitable." The Greek word translated "unprofitable" means to go bad, to become sour like milk does. "Garbage" is a good rendition of it. None does a good such as moral goodness, integrity, or kindness. No, "not even up to one." Start counting. Not ten, not even up to one—a zero.

Second, Paul speaks as a physician (vv. 13-14). He sees men's mouths or words as having the foul odor of a newly opened grave. Their tongues are deceitful. The Hebrew reads, "They smoothed their tongues"—oily, but deceitful. The imperfect tense of the verb "used deceit" means a habitual action. "The poison of asps is under their lips" (v. 13). The asp here is an Egyptian cobra, a deadly serpent. The poison lies in a bag under the lips. Such men's mouths are full of cursing and bitterness (v. 14).

Third, Paul speaks as a historian (vv. 15–18). The path of man is marked by shed blood, destruction, and misery. This suggests man's warlike nature. He has never known the way of peace but continually treads the way of violence. Furthermore, in his rebellious nature he has no fear of God.

This entire description shows how man's spirit, body, and will are captivated by evil. Barclay quotes Vaughan to the effect that these verses describes three things: "(i) A *character* whose characteristics are ignorance, indifference, crookedness and unprofitableness. (ii) A *tongue* whose notes are destructive, deceitful, malignant. (iii) A *conduct* whose marks are oppression, injuriousness, implacability. These things are the result of disregard of God" (p. 55). What a condemnation of human nature without God!

Having shown his readers their image in God's mirror, Paul makes a summary and then draws a conclusion (vv. 19–20). In the first place, Paul and his readers really know as a conviction of soul (*oidamen*) that whatever the law *says,* it speaks to the ones in the sphere of (*en*) the law (v. 19). Usually "the law" refers to the Mosaic code. However, since the description in verses 10–18 includes a passage from Isaiah, it certainly includes that also. Jews referred to their Scriptures as "the law and the prophets"; so certainly Paul is speaking of Jews.

However, so far he has cited various forms of law: nature, heart, and writings. Thus here we may see "the law" as including all these. This is evident in the words "In order that every single mouth may be stopped, and may become under judgment [liable to be tried and/or pay the penalty] every single part of the world before God" (v. 19, literal). This includes Jews and Gentiles.

Of interest are the two Greek words used for "saith." The first means the substance of what is spoken; the latter refers to the act of speaking. So the thing spoken becomes a liability upon those who live in the sphere of the law. No one can open his mouth to speak in his defense before God's judgment seat. To charge God with unfairness is not enough (see v. 26). To say that one did his best is not sufficient (see v. 23). Outside of Christ one can only stand mute and condemned to hear the awful, eternal sentence of hell. That which is "unprofitable" is thrown into Gehenna. If you are unfit for heaven, you leave God no choice but to consign you to hell—by your own choice!

Second, Paul draws a conclusion. "Therefore by the deeds of

the law there shall no flesh be justified in his sight: for by the law is the knowledge of sin" (v. 20).

In this verse "law" both times is without the definite article in the Greek; so it means "legalism." This certainly includes the Mosaic law, but it also includes the laws in nature and those written in the hearts of pagans. Failure at even one point of law means that no man (flesh) can be declared righteous in God's eyes. For through law is the full knowledge of sin. The law as God's standard of conduct serves only to cause men to know for a certainty that they are lost sinners.

With this verse Paul concludes the first section of his treatment of the gospel. He has shown conclusively man's failure to achieve the righteousness of God and that he abides under the wrath of God, however, he does not end his thought here. Instead of despair there is hope. Though men in their own power dwell in darkness, there is light breaking in the eastern sky. Men may dwell in death in their sin, but life is provided for all who will receive it. Paul sees that the "sun (Son) of righteousness" has risen with healing in his wings (see Mal. 3:2). For that reason he begins a new theme of the gospel—God has acted on man's behalf to do for him what he, anyone else, or anything else could not do for himself. That is the essence of grace. Having shown man's need of the gospel, Paul now gives his exposition of it.

The Means of Justification (3:21–31)

Since man has made such a debacle of himself (see vv. 10–18), by what means could a holy, righteous God declare such people as justified before him? This Paul treats in verses 21–31.

In verse 21 he declares, "But now." "But" is adversative, setting that which follows in contrast to what has been said up to this point. "Now" draws a curtain across the past and opens one to the present and future. The past is behind men. No longer does God deal with them according to law, except that it makes them conscious of sin (see 7:7–13). Henceforth, he deals with men by grace through faith (see vv. 22, 24).

"But now apart from law God's righteousness has been fully made manifest" (v. 21, literal). The perfect passive form means that by God it has been manifested and stands so manifested. Note that it is apart from any form of legalism. Keep in mind the meaning of *righteousness* in Romans (see 1:17). Since man within himself could not achieve the righteousness demanded by God, God has provided in Christ the God-kind-of-righteousness. Even though man is not righteous within himself, God chooses to see him as such in Christ.

Actually, this purpose of God is nothing new. For "the law and the prophets" (Old Testament) give witness to it. It was there all the time if men had only seen it (see Isa. 53), but now in Christ it is fully revealed. It is God's righteousness made available to all but is effected only "through faith in Jesus Christ" (v. 22). There is no difference in God's sight between Jew and Gentile, good and bad. It is necessary for all; it is available to all. The "faith" mentioned here is not Christ's faith but man's faith in Christ. It means belief, trust, and commitment. One believes *about* Christ, trusts *in* him, and commits himself *to* him. This is more than intellectual assent to the facts about Jesus Christ. It must reach down into the will and involve the entire person. The righteousness is offered "unto all" and comes "upon all" those who believe in Christ. The best texts do not have "upon all," but the sense is implied in "the ones believing" which qualifies "unto all."

Yes, there is no difference. "For all sinned, and keep on falling short of the glory of God." There is no difference or distinction made between Jew and Gentile: both sinned and need a Savior; there is but one Savior for both.

The Greek word translated "sinned" is a verb which means to miss the mark. Its corresponding Hebrew verb means the same. These are the most commonly used verbs in the Bible for "sin." The figure is that of failing to hit a target. The target in this case is "the glory of God." This is not a glory once possessed but lost. It is a glory not yet attained. In this context it corresponds to God's righteous nature. "Sinned" is what is called a constative aorist tense. It gives a panoramic view of the human race as doing nothing but sinning. "Come short" is the translation of the Greek verb that means being left behind as in a race, to fail to reach the goal or to fall short of it.

There are two ways to miss a target: through bad aim or through lack of power to carry the projectile to its intended mark. The former case suggests those who have the wrong concept of God's glory or righteous character. The latter pictures one who takes dead aim upon this goal, say, with an arrow, but the bowstring (a person's personal efforts) lacks the power to drive the arrow into the target. Losing power, the arrow falls to the ground short of the target. Both ideas are suggested, but the context (v. 23) favors the latter. By the works of law shall no one be declared righteous in God's sight (see v. 20). For this very reason God revealed his righteousness in Christ.

God never condemns sin but that he offers man a way out. So in verse 24 Paul hastens to add, "Being justified [declared righteous] freely by his grace through the redemption [full redemption] that is in Christ Jesus." God cannot condone sin;

so he can declare one righteous only through the redemption that is wrought "in the sphere of Christ Jesus." "Justified" or "declared righteous" actually is a term used in court; so by his judicial decree God declares righteous those who are "in Christ" through faith in him. As previously noted, this does not mean that one is personally righteous in the sense that God is righteous, but in Christ, God chooses to regard man as such.

The word *redemption* comes from the language of the slave market. It means paying the price necessary for the slave's freedom, so God in Christ paid the price necessary to free us from slavery to sin. This does not mean that the price was paid to the devil; if that were the case, the devil would be greater than God. God paid the price to himself in order to satisfy the demands of his holy, righteous nature. Since the wages of sin is death, the redemption price was the atoning death of God's Son.

Now all this becomes man's when he receives Christ as Savior. He receives it "freely by his grace." "Freely" means "for nothing"—gratis, gratuitously, without a just cause, or paying a commensurate value. A colloquial expression would be "free for nothing." It is a gift of God's "grace." The Greek word translated "grace" basically means "charm," but in usage it came to mean to make a gift, to forgive a debt, to forgive a wrong, to forgive sin. So forgiveness of sin is a free gift from God. Though it cost God everything, it costs the believing sinner nothing (see 1 Pet. 1:18–19). However, as Paul shows in Romans 6, grace, while free, makes its demands.

Verses 25–26 show how God has accomplished this. "Whom" refers to Christ Jesus. "Hath set forth" means to place before, to set forth to be looked at, to expose to public view. The Lamb slain from the foundation of the world, according to God's eternal purpose (Eph. 3:11), was exposed to public view in the arena of history that all might see in him the full revelation of God's redeeming grace and love.

He was exposed to public view as "a propitiation through faith in his blood." Since blood is identified with life, Christ gave his life that those dead in sin might have life (see John 10:11, 15, 17–18). Leviticus 17:11 reads, "For the life of the flesh is in the blood: . . . for it is the blood that maketh an atonement for the soul" (or "atonement, by reason of the life"). The life given makes atonement in order for the life to be saved.

Through the centuries much theological debate has raged as to the meaning of "propitiation" (*hilastērion*). Moody has a good discussion of this debate. He notes that the Greek form of the word here is an adjective. It describes what is done or God's redeeming work (pp. 183–84). Robertson notes its only other New Testament use is in Hebrews 9:5 where it is used as a noun and clearly means "mercy seat," but he denies that meaning for Romans 3:25. He cites examples of inscriptions found by Adolf Deissmann where as an adjective *propitiation* means "a votive offering" or "propitiatory gift." Hence Deissmann sees the use in Romans 3:25 as "The crucified Christ is the votive gift of the Divine Love for the salvation of men" (Robertson, pp. 183–84).

However, to me a votive offering hardly satisfies the weight of meaning in this passage. I cannot get away from the idea of the Day of Atonement in this verse. For instance, "to declare his righteousness for the remission of sins that are past" suggests the idea of each Day of Atonement atoning for the sins of the previous year. Hebrews 9:21–28 shows that Christ's once-for-all sacrifice fulfilled this day and its meaning, not simply for past sins but for all sins. Central in the ceremony on the Hebrew Day of Atonement was the sprinkling of the blood of sacrifice upon the mercy seat in the Holy of Holies. Only the high priest himself saw this. Fulfilled in Christ's death was this sprinkling of blood on the mercy seat. This was exposed for all to see. In this light, therefore, I see no valid reason why the rendering in Hebrews 9:5 should not apply here. Christ is both the sacrifice and the eternal high priest sprinkling his blood on the mercy seat. While pagan use of Greek words often helps us in understanding their New Testament use, it is also true that the Christian writers at times took these words and gave them a meaning all their own in keeping with the gospel. This seems to be the case here. It seems to complete Paul's figures in verses 24–25: the court of the judge or sovereign, the marketplace of the slave, and the mercy seat of the sinner (see Moody, p. 184). However one may view the meaning of *propitiation*, it certainly means that in Christ God has provided a ground for forgiveness of sin.

Now how did God actually do this in history? The answer is seen in verse 26. He "showed his righteousness in the now time, with a view to be with respect to himself just and justifier of the one whose faith is in Jesus" (literal). In the Old Testament Day of Atonement the people never actually saw what the high priest did in the Holy of Holies, but God's complete atonement in Christ was shown to all as it was exposed to public view. Thus God proved himself both "just and the justifier" of all who believe in his Son.

In his life as Christ in flesh, Jesus showed that God is *just* in his demand for righteousness in men. He lived in a body of flesh (see John 1:14) in a corrupt world. He was tempted in all points just as we are, yet he was without sin (see Heb. 4:15). As in the wilderness temptations, he was tempted in his humanity and resisted in his humanity (see Matt. 4:1–11; Luke 4:1–13). He successfully resisted temptation through prayer and meditation, through the use of Scripture, through the power of the Holy Spirit, and in total commitment to God's will. Other than the fact that he had no antecedent sin to make him susceptible to yielding, he used only that which is available to any man who is tempted. Had he not had the power to yield, his temptation would not have been real. But he also had the power not to yield. Someone said that for Jesus to live in a body of flesh with all its drives, to live in a corrupt social order, and to be tempted as he was and not sin is as great a miracle in the moral realm as his virgin birth is a miracle in the biological realm.

Thus he proved God *just* in his demand upon men for righteousness. Should a lost soul at the judgment bar accuse God of injustice in making an impossible demand which no man can meet, God will point to his Son, saying, "One did. And if he did then all men could do so." Thus men will be without excuse; every mouth will be stopped.

Then, having proved God just, Jesus was made sin (2 Cor. 5:21). In his death he paid the price for sin. Thus God became the *justifier*. For "God was in Christ, reconciling the world unto himself" (2 Cor. 5:19). Note, however, this does not automatically avail for all men. It is for those who believe in Jesus.

Then in Romans 3:27–31 through a series of questions and answers Paul concludes this portion of his debate with his imaginary questioner. "Where then is the boasting" or glorying? The Jew boasted or gloried in the fact that God was his alone (see 2:17). "It is excluded" or completely shut out. "By what law" is he justified? The law "of works?" "Nay, but by the law of faith." "Nay" (*ouchi*) is a strong negative. This law calls for faith, not works. "Therefore we conclude that a man is justified by faith without [apart from] the deeds of the law." The Greek here has no definite article with "law," so the meaning is "of law" whether the Mosaic code or any other legal code. "Conclude" means to draw a conclusion through reason.

"Is he the God of the Jews only?" Again Paul answers with the strong negative *ouchi*. He is also the God of the Gentiles. God is one God. He justifies the circumcision (Jews) "by [out of] faith" as the source and the uncircumcision (Gentiles) "through [*dia*] faith" as the intermediary instrumentality of faith. Denney (p. 614) says that both of these expressions mean the same thing. It is a kind of Hebrew parallelism by which to say the same thing in different words.

"Do we then make void the law through faith?" "Make void" means to render inoperative. Then comes Paul's familiar "God forbid." "Yea, we establish the law" ("law" again is without the definite article). The primary reference is to the Mosaic code, but it includes all forms of legalism. To "establish" the law is to put it on its proper footing. Even in the Old Testament law is related to faith (see Hab. 2:4). Abraham was saved by faith, as Paul presently shows in chapter 4. Chapters 6–8 also show that the just demands of the law are fulfilled in believers only.

Apparently Jews accused both Jesus and Paul of destroying the law (see Acts 21:20–24). Jesus himself said that not even the smallest work in the law would be done away until all be fulfilled and that he came not to destroy but to fulfill the law (see Matt. 4:17–19).

Paul saw the gospel not as opposed to Judaism but as its fulfillment, but he was also aware that only by faith in the power of the Holy Spirit can one fulfill the righteous demands of the law. He saw Christ as the end or logical goal (*telos*) of the law and love as the fulfillment of the law (see Rom. 8:4; 10:4; 13:10). Such a love is the fruit of God's provision for righteousness through the gospel.

4

The Righteousness of God Portrayed

Romans 4:1–25

In Romans 2–3 Paul employed a purely logical method of proving that both Jew and Gentile must be saved by grace through faith, not by legalism and ritualism. Of course, he referred to the Day of Atonement (3:25) but in a veiled way. Now in chapter 4 he plainly selects the case of Abraham to prove his point. He could not have chosen a better example by which to show how the God-kind-of-righteousness works because Abraham was the forefather of the Jews according to the flesh and their concept of the embodiment of faith. However, Paul refutes the Jews' claim to special privilege before God simply because they were descendants of Abraham (see Matt. 3:9). Like John the Baptist he shows that the only true child of Abraham is the one who believes in Jesus Christ.

The Justification of Abraham (4:1–8)

For his purpose, Paul selected one event out of the middle of the patriarch's life as an example of being declared righteous through faith (see Gen. 15:1–6), even though Abraham had long before this incident responded to Jehovah's call to leave his homeland and to make a journey of faith into a land yet unnamed (see Gen. 11:31–12:1; Heb. 11:8–10). "What shall we say then that Abraham our father, as pertaining to the flesh, hath found?" (v. 1). Note that Paul continues his debate with an imaginary Jewish questioner. "Father" should read "forefather." Note also that Paul refers to Abraham as "our forefather according to flesh." He uses this figure deliberately, for it puts him on equal ground with his opponent up to a point. The form of the question suggests that he anticipated an objection to the effect that he did not include faith in their relation to Abraham. The verb translated "hath found" is a perfect tense of completeness. Abraham had found one thing and nothing more, and the context implies finding by his own efforts because that is the idea Paul is refuting.

Proceeding to answer his own question Paul says, "For if

Abraham were justified by [out of, as the source] works, he hath whereof to glory; but not before God" (v. 2). The "if" clause calls for an affirmative answer. Certainly Paul did not believe this, but he used it for purposes of debate. We might translate it, "assuming that Abraham was justified out of works."

This was the claim made by the Jews. In Ecclesiasticus, a noncanonical writing, the writer praised Abraham because "he kept the law of the Most High" (44:20). Second Esdras, another such writing, suggests justification either by works or faith (9:7) or works and faith (13:23; see Moody, p 187). The Jews even claimed that Abraham performed more good works than were necessary for his own salvation. Therefore, Jews could draw upon this overabundance in order to contribute to their own salvation. This is the concept that John the Baptist denies in Luke 3:8 (see Matt. 3:9). It is of interest to note the similar view of Roman Catholics with respect to the "saints." Paul opposed this and also both positions stated in 2 Esdras.

There is no "whereof" in the Greek text which reads, "He has ground for boasting, but not before God." Abraham deserves all the credit men may accord him, but his relation to God rests upon something else entirely. Regardless of what men may say about Abraham, "What does the Scripture say?" (v. 3).

Then Paul quotes Genesis 15:6: "Abraham believed God, and it was counted unto him for righteousness." Some may insist that believing involves a work on man's part. If so, it should be noted that the ability to believe is a work of God in man. It is not a work which man does in his own strength. Paul argues against this idea. Actually belief is trust in and commitment to God by the power of the Holy Spirit working in man; so belief is itself a work of God. Now it is true that in his free will man can refuse to believe, but that is the work of Satan. Believing is the submission of man's will to God's will, and this is possible only in the power of the Holy Spirit. "Counted" is God's sovereignty; "believed" is the response of man's free will.

The key word in this verse is "counted." The Greek verb was used in bookkeeping for the act of accounting or entering into the ledger. In a sense as the result of Abraham's act of faith in God's word, God wrote across the ledger page containing Abraham's record "RIGHTEOUSNESS." This does not mean that he was perfectly righteous; his record in Genesis shows us he was not. It does mean that God chose to regard him as such.

Since this righteousness is in Christ, it must be concluded that Abraham and other Old Testament saints were saved looking forward to Christ's redeeming work, even as we in faith look back to it. In this sense we can understand why Abraham saw in prospect Messiah's day and rejoiced (see John 8:56).

In verses 4–5 Paul says that the reward of one relying upon works of law is not "accounted according to grace but according to debt." However, to the one not depending upon his own work, but believing on the one justifying the ungodly, his faith is accounted unto righteousness. The reward is a *gift* of God, not a *payment* for services rendered. The Greek verb translated "worketh" means to do that from which something results. The result is "reward" (*misthos*), dues paid for work, wages. "Debt" is that which is just or legally due. That which one expects to receive is not a gift (grace) but payment of a debt. The person who expects a gift says that God owes him something, which, of course, is not true.

If such were true, man would be under no obligation to thank or praise God for declaring him justified. God, to the contrary, would be legally obligated to him and should thank him for a job well done. On the other hand, man would have to be perfectly just to be declared just by God, and this Paul has shown to be impossible (see 3:20). Someone said that all the self-made people he knew stopped before they finished the job. This would certainly be true in this case. It is precisely for this reason that man must be saved by grace through faith in God in Christ. Faith is the channel through which God's grace flows into the believer's life. If God bestows the gift as unmerited favor (grace), then man must boast or glory in God, not in himself. This is what Abraham did, and it is what everyone who would be a true son of Abraham through faith must do. He must exercise the same faith that Abraham exercised.

In support of his example of Abraham, Paul quotes David in Psalm 32:1–2. This psalm was written after Psalm 51 (see Rom. 3:4). God had forgiven David's sins in connection with Bathsheba and her husband, Uriah; so David avows the blessed state of one who is forgiven. He was forgiven, not through his works, but through repentance and faith. On that basis his sins were covered, and God put down to his account "righteousness." When we recall David's sins of adultery and murder, then no matter how grievous our sins, we should not despair. God's grace is greater than our sins. It's application waits only for our repentance and faith. Abraham's sin was far less than David's in degree. He doubted God's promise about an heir. David went far beyond that to a sin of passion and then calculated murder. But both David and Abraham were accounted as righteous when they met God's condition.

The Futility of Circumcision (4:9–12)

Having cited David, Paul now returns to his main theme of
Abraham and his justification by faith. In order to understand
his argument in verses 9–15, you should first read Galatians 3.
This is especially true when Paul treats the matter of law in
verses 13–15.

This blessedness mentioned by David and by Paul is also at-
tributed to Abraham. Does it come "upon the circumcision only,
or upon the uncircumcision also? for we say that faith was
reckoned to Abraham for righteousness" (v. 9). There is no
"only" in the Greek text, but "also" calls for the idea. Does God
account circumcision for righteousness? Is this blessedness for
Jews alone? Or is it for Gentiles also? Of course, the Jews insisted that the former was true, but Paul denies this and insists that faith, not circumcision, is the ground for this judicial
decree of God with respect to righteousness.

To support his assertion, the apostle raises the question as to
how this righteousness was "reckoned" or put down to Abraham's account (v. 10). Note that Paul continues to debate the
issue with his imaginary questioner. Was Abraham accounted
as righteous before or after he was circumcised? Obviously it
was *before* God gave him the rite of circumcision. Genesis 15:6
speaks of God entering righteousness into his ledger record on
the basis of Abraham's faith. The giving of the rite of circumcision is recorded in Genesis 17:10–14. So as a matter of time,
righteousness preceded *circumcision*. Indeed, it was at least
fourteen years after Genesis 15:6 that the rite of circumcision
was given (see Gen. 16:16; 17:1). Thus even though the Jews
placed such value upon circumcision, Paul clearly shows that
it was not the cause of Abraham's being declared justified by
God.

Therefore, in verse 11 the apostle concludes from this se-
quence of events that Abraham is also the father of the uncircumcised. Indeed, if we press the point, he was the father of
uncircumcised believers *before* he was the father of circumcised believers. In so speaking Paul does not exclude Jewish
believers (v. 12), but he is simply showing that Abraham is the
father in faith of all, Jews and Gentiles alike, who have believed in Jesus Christ for salvation. This relationship is determined by a circumcision of the heart through faith and not
merely by the outward circumcision of the flesh (see 2:28–29),
however, it should be noted that in the Christian sense these
are children of God. Paul's point is to show that whereas Abra-

ham was justified before God prior to circumcision, so circumcision is not a prerequisite to salvation through faith as even some Christian Jews (Judaizers) insisted (see Acts 15:1; Gal. 2:2-12; 3:3; 5:2-3).

The Futility of Law (4:13-15)

Since law was another issue with respect to God's righteousness, Paul proceeds to show that Abraham was declared righteous long before the Mosaic law was given. The occasion in Genesis 15:6 was Abraham's response to God's promise to give him an heir born in his old age and that his descendants should be as numerous and uncountable as the stars (see Gen. 15:5). It was this promise that Abraham believed and which God put down to his account as righteousness.

Therefore, in verse 13 Paul declares that this promise was not made "through law, but through a righteousness of faith." In Galatians 3:16 Paul identified this "seed" (singular) of Romans 4:13 as Christ; so this innumerable host would be not Jews as such, but Jews and Gentiles who become children of God through faith in his Son.

"Heir of the world" (v. 13) refers to the kingdom or rule of God in men's hearts rather than to political rule. The Jews thought of the Messiah as a political-military figure who would overthrow their enemies, establish his reign in Jerusalem, and with whom they would rule the world. Paul elevated this idea to the level of Christian truth. "Heirs of the world" are those who in faith will be found throughout the world (see Matt. 5:5).

This promise is related to faith, not law (v. 14). If this heirship be related to the law, then faith "is completely emptied" (perfect passive) of meaning, and the promise which was related to faith "is rendered inoperative" because the law works or results in "wrath" (*orgē*, see 1:18). If there be no law, then there is no transgression. "There is no responsibility for the violation of a non-existent law" (Robertson, p. 352). Paul is not saying that God's law has no place in men's affairs. He is simply showing that neither Abraham nor anyone else is justified by keeping the law. The law has its place in making men conscious of sin. Otherwise, there would be no sense of need for being declared righteous by God through faith. But there is a limit to what law can do. When it has done its work, faith must take over to complete God's saving purpose. As Moody says, "*Law* goes with *transgression* and *wrath,* not faith and promise" (p. 189). Robertson notes that in verses 13-17 "Paul employs the key words of his gospel (faith, promise, grace) and arrays them against the current Jewish theology (law, works, merit)" (p. 352).

In Galatians 3, Paul deals with this matter more at length and points out that God's promise to Abraham, which he believed unto being declared righteous, came four hundred and thirty years before the giving of the Mosaic law (v. 17). The problem of the Jews was that they placed their emphasis upon the Mosaic covenant of law rather than on the Abrahamic covenant of grace. In verse 17 Paul says that the covenant of grace "was confirmed before of God in Christ" (literal). The Mosaic covenant "cannot disannul" the Abrahamic covenant and thus make the promise to Abraham and his seed (Christ, Gal. 3:16) of no effect. The Mosaic covenant was not a *saving* but a *serving* covenant. God's purpose to save all who believe in Christ is expressed in the covenant of grace through faith made with Abraham. The confusion of the place and purpose of these two covenants has resulted in much bad theology and serious misunderstanding as to what is involved in the plan of salvation. Confusion in both areas is with us even today.

The Type of Justification (4:16-25)

In this section Paul illustrates his illustration. Since Abraham's faith was entered into God's ledger as righteousness, how was this done? What is its meaning for Paul's original readers and for us (see vv. 23-25)?

Having treated the question of circumcision and law with respect to Abraham's experience, in verses 16-17 Paul draws a conclusion.

"Therefore" introduces this conclusion growing out of the preceding argument (v. 16). Abraham's experience was "of [out of] faith" as the source and "by [according to] grace" as the pattern. That is so that the promise might be guaranteed (sure) to all of Abraham's seed: not to those only who live by the law, but to those who live by faith. Paul is not saying that Jews are saved by law and Gentiles by faith. This would be contrary to his whole argument. The fact is he denies that anyone can be saved by the law and affirms that all must be saved by faith, for Abraham is "the father of all" who believe, that is, he is the spiritual father of all believers in Christ (see Acts 15:11).

In verse 17 Paul quotes Genesis 17:5 in support of the closing words of verse 16, but he hastens to add that this fatherhood is based upon faith. After this parenthetical quotation he resumes the thought of verse 16.

"He is the father of us all [Jewish and Gentile believers] . . .
before him whom he believed, even God, who quickeneth the
dead, and calleth those things which be not as though they
were" (vv. 16–17). While Abraham is called the father of all
true believers in the sense that they exercise a similar but personal faith, Paul infers by his reference to God that all believers, including Abraham, have God as their Father. "Before
him" is the translation of a Greek word meaning "right in front
of" as believers standing before God.

To Paul, faith means faith *in* God. It is not simply faith in
faith or faith *about* God or Christ. It is faith *in* God, in Christ.
In 2 Timothy 1:12 the King James Version reads, "For I know
whom I have believed," but the Greek text reads "in whom."
The entire verse carries a banking sense. "That which I have
committed" is the translation of three Greek words meaning
"the thing placed alongside belonging to me." A better reading is
"my deposit." You can read a bank's statement of assets and
liabilities and believe about the bank that it is solvent, but you
believe in the bank when you place your money there on deposit.

This is the kind of faith of which Paul speaks in Romans
4:17. Abraham believed in God and his promise that he could
make alive his and Sarah's bodies that they might have a son,
that God could call into being those things which seemed not
to be. Moody (p. 190) notes that this idea was prevalent in current Judaism. "With a word thou callest into life that which was
not, and with mighty power thou rulest that which has not yet
come to be" (2 Baruch 48:8, a noncanonical writing). Abraham certainly had such a faith in God. This brings us to the
heart of Paul's explanation of his illustration of Abraham's
faith.

In spite of all human reason to the contrary, Abraham believed God's promise to give him an heir (v. 18). The birth of
Isaac was like life from the dead or a resurrection, and the
multitude of Abraham's seed was like speaking of things which
did not exist as though they did: "Who against hope believed
in hope." This is the nature of the patriarch's faith and literally
means, "who beyond hope believed upon hope." Abraham was
beyond or past hope of having a child by Sarah, yet he fastened
his faith upon the hope which he had in God's promise that he
would be the father of many nations (note the plural) and
would have innumerable seed.

Abraham might be weak in body but not in faith (v. 19).
The negative "not" after "considered" is not in the best Greek
texts. Abraham set his mind upon the matter and knew that

genetically his body was "completely dead" (perfect tense).
He had no natural hope of procreation. The perfect participle
means that his body in this regard was dead. It had ceased to
function in this way and never would again. He also squarely
faced Sarah's situation and knew that the same was true of her.
At the time he was "about an hundred years old" and Sarah
was ninety.

This condition was enough to stagger anyone's faith; yet
Abraham "staggered not at the promise of God through unbelief" (v. 20). The Greek text places the emphasis upon the
promise. "With respect to the promise of God Abraham did
not stagger in unbelief" or in "no faith." "Staggered" is the translation of a Greek verb meaning to judge between two things. On
the one hand, there was God's promise. On the other hand,
there were his and Sarah's bodies. Which should he believe?
That which he knew to be true about their bodies or God's
promise? He did not vacillate or stagger. Despite what he knew
about himself and Sarah, Abraham also knew the power of
God; so he "believed God," or he "believed in God." He was
strong in faith and gave glory to God. What he and Sarah could
not do, God could do; so he committed the matter to God. It
was all of God and none of them. So to God be the glory!

Abraham was fully assured that what God had promised, he
had the power to do (v. 21). His faith did not revitalize his
procreative powers but led him to put the entire matter in
God's hands. Like the birth of John the Baptist, Isaac's birth
was a biological miracle. It was not a virgin birth, of course,
but it was a supranatural one.

However, as I read Paul's words here, I cannot help thinking
of the angel's words to Mary. Speaking of Elisabeth's coming
motherhood, Gabriel said, "For with God nothing shall be impossible" (Luke 1:37). Literally, "For alongside, or in the presence of, God not any single word is impossible." (In the Greek
the negatives come first for emphasis—"For not impossible.
. . .") What God says, he can do!

Abraham believed this. "And therefore it was imputed to
him [put down to his account] for righteousness" (Rom. 4:22).
He looked, not at God through the problem, but at the problem
through God, and his faith was equal to the occasion.

Paul concludes this chapter by relating the experience of
Abraham to his readers then and for all time. This was not an
isolated event of one man's experience with God. It was not for
Abraham's sake alone that his faith was accounted to him
(v. 23). "For righteousness" is not in the best texts, but the
context calls for it. It was written "for us also" (v. 24). Paul

qualifies this by adding "to whom it is about to be accounted, to the ones believing upon the one raising Jesus our Lord out of the realm of the dead" (literal).

The phrase "shall be imputed" is not a future tense in the Greek text but a present tense (*mellei*) with an infinitive to indicate that something is about to happen. "It is about to be accounted" as righteousness. Denney (p. 621) says, *"Mellei* conveys the idea of a Divine order under which things proceed so."* "If we believe" expresses a condition, but the Greek text reads, "To the ones believing." This naturally follows "to whom." Denney translates it "believing as we do." Paul assumes that his readers, along with him, have the same faith as was found in Abraham, but this idea may also be extended to include all such believers.

Abraham believed that God was able to bring life out of the dead—his and Sarah's *dead* bodies insofar as procreation was concerned—but Paul relates present faith to God's power shown as he raised "Jesus our Lord" from the dead. Of course, this implies God's omnipotence, but Christian faith is not centered in that alone. It is in God's omnipotent act in raising Jesus from the dead. Thus it is centered in a person, the crucified, risen, and living Lord Jesus (see 5:10). What to man is impossible is possible with God, and Paul's words relate this almightiness to the spiritual realm in his reference to Jesus' resurrection. God's omnipotence is rooted in God's eternal redemptive purpose.

The apostle further explains this in verse 25. "Who was delivered for our offences [fallings aside, transgressions], and was raised again for our justification," our being declared righteous before God. Had Jesus merely died on a cross he would have been only one of a multitude that did so. Unlike the others, however, he was raised from the dead. This makes him unique. Furthermore, it means that his death was redemptive.

The Greek verb translated "delivered" means "given alongside." This same Greek verb is used of Judas's betraying Jesus, of the Sanhedrin's handing Jesus over to Pilate for his sentence of death, and Pilate's handing him over to the soldiers for crucifixion. However, in verse 25 it refers to God's handing the Son over to be crucified, to die redemptively, that he might pay the penalty for human sin. Then God raised him from the dead "for our justification." It was the resurrection that made the difference between Jesus' death and all others. In 1 Corinthians 15:3–4 Paul summarizes the gospel. "Christ died for our sins according to the scriptures; . . . he rose again the third day according to the scriptures."

The faith experience of Abraham suggests another thought. Paul speaks of lost people as "dead in trespasses and sins" (Eph. 2:1) who through faith in Christ "are quickened [made alive] together with Christ" (Eph. 2:5). A lost person brought under conviction sees himself as dead. He recognizes the enormity of his guilt. Human reason tells him that his case is hopeless, but in faith he sees the power of God; so *against* hope he believes *in* or *upon* hope. Knowing God's promise to save all who believe in his Son, he does not vacillate, but he is strong in faith to believe that what he, anyone else, or anything else cannot do for him, God in Christ can do. He casts himself in trust and commitment upon God's grace. He stands in the long line of Abraham's faith, and thus it is accounted unto him as righteousness. Unrighteous within himself, he receives the righteousness of God which is in Christ.

Whether Jew or Gentile, therefore, he becomes a child of God. This is what the gospel is all about.

5

The Saving Grace of God

Romans 5:1–21

Up to this point Paul's emphasis has been upon justification, but in the next four chapters he turns his thoughts to salvation, which is the natural result of justification. The believer is declared justified before God through his faith in Jesus Christ. As noted earlier *righteousness* in Romans refers to that state which God declares to be that of the believer. Even though the believer is not righteous as God is righteous, God wills to regard him as such through the righteousness which is in his Son.

In chapter 5 great emphasis is placed upon reconciliation. In Christ and his atoning work, that which separates the sinner from God is removed by God's grace through the believer's trust in and commitment to Christ. Never does the Bible say that God needs to be reconciled to man; rather man needs to be reconciled to God. Otherwise, there would be no offer of salvation. In Christ a loving God has provided the means whereby rebellious man may be brought back into God's fellowship, and that is provided by God's grace through faith (see Eph. 2:8).

The Nature and Need of Grace (5:1–11)

Though the word *grace* is not used until verse 2, it is evident throughout the chapter. Grace is the source of God's salvation; faith is the channel of that salvation.

"Therefore" (v. 1) refers to what Paul has said in Romans 4. Abraham was justified by faith, not by works, circumcision, or legalism. On this basis Paul assumes that his readers also have been "justified by faith" or out of faith. As Wuest (p. 75) says, the last three do not give one peace. Only faith does this. "Peace" is that inner state of *accounted righteousness* which enables us to stand "face to face" (*pros*) with God with no fear of his wrath or universal, abiding opposition to evil (*orgē*, see 1:18). And we have this peace "through [*dia*, immediate agency] our Lord Jesus Christ." No man can stand before God in peace growing out of his own merit. It is on the basis of

Christ's merit. This is one sense of Paul's often used phrase
"in Christ."

Romans 5:1 in the King James Version reads, "We have
peace" (see also RSV). Interpreters differ as to the true reading
here, and the disagreement is derived from one Greek letter.
Should "have" read *echomen* or *echōmen*? Note that the only
difference in spelling is a short *o* (omicron) or a long *ō*
(omega). To the average reader this may seem like splitting a
hair, but careful textual study deals in such things. If the
reading has the short *o*, it is a present indicative stating a fact:
"we have peace." If the long *ō* be used, it is a present active subjunctive, "Let us have peace," and thus becomes an exhortation. The latter reading has the weight of scholarship behind
it (William Barclay, Edgar J. Goodspeed, James Moffatt, James
Denney, Eberhard Nestle, A. T. Robertson, William Sanday and
Arthur Headlam, Konstantin von Tischendorf). Erwin Nestle in
the sixteenth edition of his father's work (*Novum Testamentum
Graece*, Greek New Testament) uses *echomen* in the text and
places *echōmen* as a footnote, thus reversing his father's usage.
The fact that "we have access" and "we stand" are indicative
modes makes one wonder about "we have" or "let us have."

Most recent commentaries, possibly following Hans Lietz-
mann (1933), agree with the grammarians on textual grounds,
but they hold that the hortatory idea is not acceptable on theological grounds. They see Paul in verses 1–2 as stating a fact,
not exhorting his readers to achieve something. Through justification by faith they already have peace with God. Denney
(p. 623), while recognizing the textual evidence for *echōmen*,
notes that "there is no indication that the Apostle has finished
his dogmatic exposition, and is proceeding to exhortation." By
careful grammatical analysis in which he notes "the uninter-
rupted series of indicatives afterwards [after v. 3]," he says
that "the logic of the situation" favors *echomen*. He also cites
other authorities to this effect (see also Wuest, pp. 75–76). For
whatever it may be worth, I agree with this position. "The justified have peace with God: *i.e.*, His wrath (1:18) no longer
threatens them; they are accepted in Christ. It is not a change
in their feelings which is indicated, but a change in God's relation to them" (Denney, p. 623).

The word translated "peace" comes from the Greek verb
meaning to bind together that which has been separated. Our
Lord made this possible between God and men through the
blood of his cross (see Col. 1:20).

"By whom [Christ] also we have access by faith into this
grace wherein we stand, and rejoice in hope of the glory of

God" (v. 2). "Have" is a perfect indicative form of *echō*, the same verb translated "have" in verse 1. The perfect tense means "we have and still have access." "Access" is the translation of a word from a compound verb *agō*, to bring, and the prefix *pros*, face to face. The verb means to bring someone into another's presence. In the Greek papyri (the records of business transactions and the letters of ordinary people that have been discovered in the last century), the verb *agō* is used meaning to present or introduce. The very word used here is found in the sense of a landing-stage as in a harbor. Wuest (pp. 77–78) mentions the sense of one bringing a friend, properly attired, into the presence and favor of the king for an audience. The French word for this is *entrée*.

This is what Jesus does for the believing sinner; now clothed in his accounted righteousness, the sinner has *entrée* into the presence of God. Cleansed by Christ's blood and clothed with Christ's righteousness, the sinner comes into God's full favor or grace. Grace is the harbor entered through faith; the believer has a landing-stage into God's presence in peace. The verb translated "stand" is also a perfect tense; so we have permanent access, and we stand as a fixed state in God's grace through faith. Thus we rejoice or glory upon the hope of the glory of God. This hope is that of sharing in the glory of heaven. Having come short of God's glory through sin (3:23), through faith we anticipate this glory in heaven.

However, the Christian faith is more than pie in the sky. It is the sustaining power of the Christian while he remains on earth. Through this faith we "come boldly unto the throne of grace, that we may obtain mercy, and find grace to help in time of need" (Heb. 4:16). Thus to saving grace God adds sustaining grace. Not only do we rejoice in the hope of glory in heaven, but we rejoice also in the assurance of help in the trials of earth (v. 3).

"We glory" (present tense) means that we keep on glorying "in tribulations." Rather than whining over tribulations, we rejoice that we are counted worthy to experience them. Paul's life is a commentary on this fact. "Tribulations" translates a word meaning pressing situations, like grapes squeezed in a winepress. Tribulation can be compared to being in a tight place with seemingly no way out. Within our own strength that may be true, but in Christ there is a way out, even if it must be through the tribulations. Jesus said, "In the world ye shall have tribulation: but be of good cheer [courage]; I have overcome [fully conquered] the world" (John 16:33).

The Christian can rejoice in tribulations because he knows

with perception or fully knows (*eidotes*) that tribulation works, or produces, "patience." This word comes from the Greek verb meaning to abide under. Rather than ask that we be spared, we endure so that our efforts result in "patience." The noun form was used in athletics and in military life for one who could take all his opponent could throw against him and still have reserve strength with which to countercharge to victory. "Experience" translates a Greek word meaning the result of testing (v. 4). The one tested is proved by patience in tribulation to be genuine. Experience has been called "approvedness" (Denney, p. 624) and "character" (RSV). This kind of character has "hope." Having seen what God can do for us in the other experiences results in hope. The verb translated "worketh" is to be understood in verse 4. "Tribulation . . . hope" Robertson calls "a linked chain." One link leads to the other, and so on to the end of the chain.

Verse 5 completes the three Christian graces with "love" (see 1 Cor. 13:13). The kind of hope resulting from Christian character "maketh not ashamed." It is neither repulsed nor deceived; rather it conquers in truth, for "the love of God is shed abroad [fully poured out, perfect passive form] in our hearts by the Holy Ghost [Spirit] which is given unto us" (v. 5). This love was poured out by God, but through the Holy Spirit he poured it into us when the Spirit indwelt us at the moment of regeneration (see John 14:17). The sense of the perfect tense (shed abroad) is that God's love still indwells the Christian through the Holy Spirit.

In verses 6–8 Paul describes the working of this love. "Without strength" (v. 6) means that outside of Christ we were powerless either to work good or to save ourselves. "In due time" means "according to time" or the opportune time (see "fulness of the time," Gal. 4:4). It was the time, not chronological but opportune, which was right in God's eyes. In such a time "Christ died for the ungodly." The word translated "ungodly" means lack of piety or reverence toward God. "Our hearts" includes both Jews and Gentiles (see 1:19–3:31); so Christ died "for" [*huper*, instead of, as a substitute for] all men. Here we definitely see the substitutionary atonement (see John 10:15; 11:50; Gal. 3:13). Christ died in our place, suffering the penalty for our sins (see Isa. 53:4–6).

Arguing from the human standpoint, Paul contrasts one's attitude toward a "righteous" and a "good man" (v. 7). "Righteous" describes one who lives by the law, expects all others to do the same, and has no sympathy for one who does not. "Good" means "benevolent," "kind," or "generous." The distinction has been drawn thus: *Righteous* means "absolutely without sympathy"; *good* means "beneficent and kind." A man would hardly die for the former, but perhaps he might have the courage to die for the latter.

"But" is adversative, contrasting God with such a man (v. 8). "God commendeth his love toward us, in that while we were yet sinners, Christ died for us." The Greek verb translated "commendeth" means to stand with or together, to put together by combining, so to prove or exhibit. It means here more than merely recommending. It carries the idea of proving or demonstrating. God's greatest demonstration of his love is seen in Christ at Calvary. Whereas an unusual man *might* die for a benevolent, kind friend, Christ died for those who were/are God's enemies. "His love" should read "his own love." One can say no more than to quote John 3:16. However, Robertson says that Christ died for us "not because we were Jews or Greeks, rich or poor, righteous or good, but plain sinners" (p. 357; see Luke 18:13). The publican's prayer reads "to me the sinner," as if he were the only sinner in the world. If you or I were the only sinner, Christ still would have died "for" (*huper*) that one who was/is lost from God.

In verse 9 Paul argues from the greater to the lesser. Since as God's enemies we are now declared just "in the sphere of his blood, we shall be saved through him from the wrath [*orgē*]" (literal). He is thinking here of the *now* and *then, then* being the final judgment. Note "the wrath," which is the "lake of fire" (Rev. 20:15) or "the second death" (Rev. 20:14). "If" in verse 10 introduces a condition assumed as true. We were God's "enemies" but now are reconciled to him by the death of his Son. "Reconciled" translates a verb which means to change or exchange; thus it connotes the act of reconciling or bringing together estranged parties. It changes their relation to one of peace. It may refer to mutual or one-sided reconciliation. In the case of God reconciling man to himself it is the latter.

Moody is helpful at this point: "In the four great Pauline passages on reconciliation there are four cardinal points: (1) God is always the subject, the one who does the reconciling; (2) man (or the world, or all things not God) is always the object, the one in need of reconciliation; (3) the death of Christ is the means; (4) and the ministry of reconciliation is the result (2 Cor. 5:18–21; Rom. 5:10–11; Col. 1:20; Eph. 2:16)" (p. 194). Reconciliation is synonymous with justification or regeneration.

Having been justified or reconciled through "the death of his Son, much more, being reconciled, we shall be saved by his

life" (v. 10), or "in the sphere of his life." "Life" is the translation of zōē, referring to spiritual life. This does not refer to
Jesus' life prior to Calvary. He is more than an example; he is
the Redeemer. Since the life is in the blood, being reconciled
by Jesus' blood and life may be seen as the same idea.
However, we are reconciled by his "blood" and "shall be
saved by his life" suggest two different things. Reconciled by
his blood or death refers to *justification* or regeneration. "Shall
be saved [future] by his life" suggests *sanctification* through his
continuing resurrection life. Of course, Jesus' resurrection made
effective his atoning death, but the words "reconciled" and
"saved" make them two separate entities.

Note that the two uses of "shall be saved" (vv. 9–10) are
both future tenses. Some see this to mean that our salvation is
not certain until the end of life or until we appear before the
judgment bar of God. However, the New Testament abundantly
teaches otherwise. The final judgment will not *determine* but
will simply *declare* whether or not we are destined for heaven
or hell. In Jesus' picture of the judgment in Matthew 25:31–46,
putting some on the right or left does not make them sheep or
goats. The sheep are placed on the right because they are
sheep; the goats are placed on the left because they are
goats. Furthermore, in the final judgment scene in Revelation 20:11–15, there is a "book" and there are the "books."
The dead will be judged "out of those things which were written
[perfect tense, written and stand written] in the books, according to their works" (Rev. 20:12). The other book is called "the
book of life" or "of the life" (see "eternal life," John 3:16).
Those who have been justified have their names in this book
and so are not cast into the lake of fire. All others are cast into
that lake. How, then, may we understand "the books" out of
which everyone is judged? No distinction is made here as to
the saved and lost. This judgment will be as to works and will
determine degrees of reward in heaven and punishment in
hell.

The use of the future tense in Romans 5:9–10 may be understood in light of the threefold nature of salvation (see 1:16):
justification (regeneration), sanctification, and glorification.
This entire passage is written within the context of justification
by faith; so the issue is not that of the saving of the soul. Since
verse 9 relates to the final judgment, "shall be saved" seems to
refer to glorification. Rather than receiving God's wrath, the
believer will partake of his glory: the sum-total of glory and
rewards in heaven, including the resurrection of the dead body
(see Rom. 6:5; 8:23, 30; Heb. 9:28). Verse 10 seems to in-

volve sanctification or the saving of the Christian life. The living Christ indwelling the believer through the Spirit enables him to live according to God's will (see John 17:17, 19; Heb. 2:3). It should be recalled that one does not grow *into* but *in* the state of sanctification which is simultaneous with justification. One should not press the point that Paul reverses the order to put glorification before sanctification. He was dictating and expressed the thoughts as they came to mind. At the same time because one is justified and is certain of glorification, he can place his life-emphasis upon his state of sanctification. This thought is further developed in chapters 7-8. One should read "redemption" or "full-redemption" in Ephesians 1:14 in light of the threefold nature of salvation.

Because of the assurance the Christian has in "God through our Lord Jesus Christ," he can glory or rejoice (v. 11). It is through God in Christ that he has now received "the reconciliation." This, rather than "atonement," is the reading of the Greek text. However, the reconciliation does result in the atonement (at-one-ment) between God and man.

The Sin and Death through Adam (5:12-14)

Paul now moves into a discussion of what Moody (p. 195) calls "The Reign of Grace" (5:12-21). He begins by showing Adam as the type of which he later shows Christ as the antitype.

"Wherefore" (v. 12) may refer to previous words (vv. 1-11) or it may simply be a transitional word in Paul's reasoning. Probably the latter is true. It does, however, connect God's act of reconciliation to the need for reconciliation. Note the uses of "one" through verse 19. The context shows whether it refers to Adam or to Christ.

"As by one man sin entered into the world, and death by sin" (v. 12). Paul, like Moses in Genesis, does not attempt to deal with the origin of evil, a subject which has baffled the greatest minds through the ages. However evil originated, its presence is evident in the world. Sin is the product of evil, but Paul simply says that "sin entered into the world." It *came* into the world through the choice of Adam and Eve to obey Satan rather than God (see Gen. 3), and "death [came] through sin." While physical death is the fruit of sin, the primary idea is spiritual death or separation from God's fellowship. God told Adam that the day he ate of the forbidden fruit he would surely die. The fact that he lived physically long after that day shows the primary idea of spiritual death.

The consequence was that death "passed" or "came through." It "spread" (RSV) to all men. The verb translated "entered" is *eiserchomai*, to come into; the verb translated "passed" is *dierchomai*, to come through. "Passed" pictures in the aorist tense the whole of the tragic experience of the race. "For that all have sinned." "Have sinned" or simply "sinned" is a constative or summary aorist tense. It summarizes the sad history of man. "For that" (because) is a translation of *eph' hōi*. Robertson notes that in the old Greek this usually meant "on condition that" (p. 358). "Because" (RSV) is a good translation. What happened to Adam has happened to all, but it is *because* all sinned.

Moody (p. 195) notes that Augustine's doctrine of original sin, or inherited guilt, resulted from his small knowledge of Greek. Thus he followed the Latin translation of *in quo* (in whom). His position is rejected today even by Roman Catholic scholars who admit that it is not in the Scripture. This does not in any sense deny the consequences in those who follow Adam's example, but it does place the burden of responsibility upon each individual person (see Jer. 31:29–30).

How, then, may we understand Paul's use of Adam and his relation to our sin and guilt? Adam was created in a state of innocence but with a tendency toward sin as shown in later developments. Originally he was neither righteous nor unrighteous. To be righteous he must have and refuse the opportunity to be unrighteous, hence his temptation experience. When faced with the choice, he chose to be unrighteous in that he obeyed Satan rather than God. His tendency toward sin led him to make this choice. Thus he sinned or missed the mark. He did not fall out of righteousness into unrighteousness. He fell from the state of innocence into unrighteousness when he committed personal sin. As Paul says in Romans 3:23, Adam fell short of, not from, the glory of God.

In this sense every person starts out in a state of innocence, but like Adam each has a tendency toward sin, and once reaching the age of accountability each chooses to follow Satan's will. Thus one becomes a personal sinner, coming short of God's glory. He is by his own free will unrighteous before God. Infants and mentally incompetents are for this reason still innocent before God, and they are somehow declared righteous by God in his grace.

Adam is often called the *federal* head of the race, meaning that all men are born in a state of lostness because of Adam's sin. This idea stems from Augustine's interpretation of original sin or inherited guilt. Its end is seen in the traditional Roman

Catholic view that those dying in infancy are in *limbo*. We have already noted that modern Roman Catholic scholars reject this position as not being supported by the Scripture.

Nothing is lost from the ultimate meaning of the sin of Adam passing through all men if we see this to mean that, like Adam, a child is born in a state of innocence, neither righteous nor unrighteous, but with a tendency toward sin. When the child reaches the age of knowledgeable personal choice and chooses evil, as all do, then he is in a state of unrighteousness or lostness. But this does agree with the dealings of God with men as revealed in the Bible. Man makes a deliberate choice of unrighteousness; so everyone is responsible for his own condition. He cannot say that either Adam or the devil made him do it. Like Adam, he made his choice in his own free will.

This view also helps to understand the wilderness temptations of Jesus. Insofar as his role as the Christ was concerned, he also was in a state of innocence—but with a tendency toward righteousness. Satan sought to deter him from God's will, even as he did with Adam. He succeeded with Adam but failed with Jesus. This was true in every one of Jesus' temptations throughout his ministry. Thus Jesus is the head or source out of which flow all who through faith in him receive the God-kind-of-righteousness.

Parenthetically (see vv. 13–17) Paul says that "until the law sin was in the world: but sin is not imputed [accounted] when there is no law" (v. 13). The sin principle was in the world before the giving of the Mosaic law. Paul, however, has shown that antedating that code was law written in the heart (see 2:12–16). So he is not saying that men were free from guilt prior to that time (see the flood). Man was responsible for the law he had, but the responsibility is greater for those who have the written law, as Paul has also shown. Moody (p. 196) is helpful at this point. The accounting of sin is God's side of the human awareness of sin. Man has inherited from Adam the tendency toward sin, but there is no guilt until he sins after he is personally aware of the difference between right and wrong (the age of accountability or the ability to discern between right and wrong).

In the Greek "law" in both cases (v. 13) is without the definite article, so it may apply to the law written in men's hearts. Adam had God's law about not eating the forbidden fruit (see Gen. 2:16–17). Had he innocently eaten it before God forbade it, there would have been no accounting of sin. But because he deliberately chose to disobey God's law, sin was put down to his account. Since God's law is written in every man's heart, no one can claim to have violated it in innocence. Sin is accounted to those who disobey the light God has given them. Of course, the greatest accounting was against those who in rebellion disregarded the Mosaic code.

Paul notes this fact in verse 14: "Nevertheless death reigned from Adam to Moses, even over them that had not sinned after the similitude of Adam's transgression, who is the figure [tupos, type] of him that was to come [Christ]."

"Death" refers primarily to spiritual death or the soul's separation from God. It reigned as king from Adam to Moses or the giving of the Mosaic law. This death is the fruit of sin, not in Adam alone, but in all men. It reigns even in those whose sinning is not like that of Adam. Adam sinned against a directly spoken law of God; others sinned against God's law in their hearts.

The apostle clearly states that Adam is a type of Christ. He is a type in the sense that both faced God's will; Adam refused it, Christ accepted it. Adam brought death; Christ gives life. Literally, "For as in the sphere of Adam all die, even so in the sphere of Christ shall all be made alive" (1 Cor. 15:22). The immediate context deals with physical death and the resurrection life, but the principle also applies in the spiritual realm (see Eph. 2:1, 5–6).

So thinking of Adam as a state of *innocence*, Moses as symbolic of *law*, and Christ as the *redeemer*, the spiritual history of God's justified ones may be written as "Adam to Moses to Christ" (Moody, p. 196). Innocent but with a tendency toward sin, man rebels against God's law and finds salvation in Christ who ever has the tendency toward righteousness. And this salvation is the gift of God's grace.

The Grace and Life through Christ (5:15–17)

If death came through the *type*, grace and life came through the *antitype*. Grace and spiritual life (*zōē*, v. 17) far surpass death.

"Offence" refers to Adam's falling aside from the path of God's will (v. 15). "The free gift" means the *charisma*, a gift of God's grace. This refers to life eternal in its fullest sense. Adam's offense resulted from his tendency toward sin. This and the resultant death, physical and spiritual, have been passed on to all men as they follow in Adam's footsteps.

Paul argues from the lesser to the greater as he says, "Much more the grace of God, and the gift [gratuitous gift, *dōrea*] by [*en*, in the sphere of] grace, which is by one man, Jesus Christ, hath abounded unto many" (v. 15), or "unto the many over-

flowed." God's grace far overflows man's sin. As out of Adam
flowed sin, judgment, and death, out of Jesus Christ overflowed
forgiveness, the state of being declared just, and spiritual life.
To paraphrase T. W. Manson's words (Moody, p. 196), "Adam
took what was forbidden; Christ gives that which is not de-
served." The offense came through "the one" (Adam); the
gratuitous gift of grace came through "the one" (Christ).

"The many" is suggestive of my comments as to Adam and
the race and to Christ and the race. The fact that Adam sinned
did not in itself make all men personal sinners. The tendency
toward sin in both resulted in personal sin for all. By the same
token the fact that in Christ God offers his gift of grace does
not mean that all receive it. It is offered to all but is actually
received by those who accept it through faith in Christ. Thus
God respects man's free will on both the debit and the credit
sides of his ledger.

Paul continues his contrast in verse 16: "And not as through
one sinning the gratuitous gift. For, on the one hand, judgment with the result of condemnation, but, on the other hand,
the free gift out of many transgressions [fallings aside] with
the result of justification" (literal). "Condemnation" is translated from the Greek *katakrima*, a judging down, which in the
papyri is never used of an acquittal. It is used in the sense of
finding guilty and pronouncing sentence. Adam and all those
who follow after him are found guilty and sentenced. On the
other hand, God's gift of grace is the result of the many sins
of Adam and his descendants. It was precisely this which resulted in salvation by grace through faith. Otherwise all men
would be lost without hope. "Justification" as acquittal is in contrast to "condemnation." God's wrath abounds against sin; his
grace abounds toward sinners; but each must accept it for himself.

Continuing his argument from the lesser to the greater (v.
17), Paul says that if by "the one" man (Adam) sin (death)
reigned as king because of "the one" (Greek), "much more the
ones receiving the overflowing of the grace and of the gratuitous
gift of the righteousness in the sphere of spiritual life shall
reign as king through the one, Jesus Christ" (literal). The Greek
includes the definite article with the three references to "one"—
"the one." The first two refer to Adam; the third refers to Christ.
Also note the repeated uses of the definite article *the* in the latter
half of the verse. The twice-used "reign" is the key thought in
the verse. Death is king outside of Christ, but those who receive
the King are *kings* in victorious Christian living.

Out of grace, one receives this life. By God's grace man lives the reigning or victorious life. The way of death and the way of life beckon to every person. Each must decide which road he will travel.

The Summary of Experience (5:18–21)

Following the parenthetical statement, Paul now returns to the incompleted thought of verse 12. However, verses 18–21 also summarize the thought expressed in the parenthetical statement. "Therefore" may read "so then," as Paul resumes the parallel between Adam and Christ begun in verse 12. Through Adam's offense condemnation (*katakrima*, see v. 16) resulted for all men. Through Christ, "righteousness of life" resulted for all men through God's declaring men righteous in Christ (v. 18). Whereas "through the disobedience of the one man the many were made [set down as] sinners, so also through the obedience of the one the many shall be made [set down as] righteous" (v. 19, literal). Note the contrasts: the one (Adam) and the one (Christ); disobedience and obedience; sinners and righteous; the many (lost) and the many (saved). Of course, the lost followed Adam by sinning personally, even as the saved partake of Christ's righteousness through their personal faith in him.

The Greek word translated "disobedience" means a hearing alongside. It connotes the idea of failing to hear, of hearing wrongly or paying no attention to what is said. In Adam's case it means active disobedience or refusal to abide by God's command. "Obedience" translates a kindred Greek word meaning to hear under or in submission to the one speaking (see Heb. 10:7). Adam's disobedience in his tendency toward sin is duplicated in man who is in the likeness of Adam. Christ's act of obedience enables all who believe in him to be declared righteous.

Before the Mosaic law, man was disobedient to the law written in his heart, but the guilt was increased for those who received the Mosaic law (v. 20). "Law" in the Greek is without the definite article. But here it evidently refers to the Mosaic law. It "entered" or came in as the result of sin entering the world (see v. 12). "Abound" here means to increase. The offense or transgression increased in nature as it was against the clearly stated law of God.

However, where "sin abounded [increased], grace did much more abound." "Abounded" is the same verb as "abound" in verse 20, but "much more abound" is the translation of a different verb. This verb is found in the New Testament only here and in 2 Corinthians 7:4. It is the verb *perisseuō*, to overflow

or to be above a certain measure, with the prefix *huper* which
in this context means upper, over, or beyond. It may read *superabounded*. When the container of God's grace was filled to the
brim, then grace overflowed beyond measure. Wuest catches
the sense of it when he translates it, "Where sin increased
[*pleonazō*], grace superabounded, and then some on top of that"
(p. 89). Sin was deluged by God's grace which is greater than
all our sins. No matter what the measure of our sins may be,
God's supply of grace is infinitely greater to forgive all who
believe in Jesus.

So Paul closes this phase of his exposition of the gospel with
a final and climactic contrast between sin and grace (v. 21).
Since both *sin* and *grace* are feminine gender in Greek, Moody
notes what has been called the "war of the two queens." "As
sin reigned as a queen in the sphere of death, so also grace
might reign as a queen through righteousness unto life eternal
through Jesus Christ our Lord" (p. 197). The result is the victory of life over death. Since this life is out of eternity, it is the
life of God given to men through the redemptive work and me-
diatorship of Christ (see John 1:12).

There is no chapter in Romans which is more important and
more difficult to interpret than chapter 5. It goes to the very
heart of the sin problem and how God deals with it in grace
through his Son. Though in a state of innocence, Adam had a
tendency toward sin. His active transgression initiated the long,
sad history of sinful men. Like Adam, every person has this inherent tendency toward sin. The traditional name for it is *de-
pravity*. When one yields to it in disobedience to God's law as
he possesses it, one becomes an active, personal transgressor.
We have seen that one can be saved by keeping God's law which
he possesses—either in his heart or in the written law. But to
do so he must keep all of it all the time, which, of course, no
man does. Thus a man is not arbitrarily fated to condemnation
simply because he is a physical descendant of Adam. He is personally guilty and condemned when spiritually he follows his
tendency toward sin even as did Adam.

At the same time we must note that God has taken the initiative in reconciling men to himself through the redemptive work
wrought through his Son. However, men are not automatically
saved because of this. As each one is condemned because of personal sin and guilt, so one is saved through personal faith in
Jesus Christ. God deals with people as individuals, not en
masse. Whether sin reigns unto condemnation or grace reigns
unto eternal life rests in the free will of man. Men are account-
able to God both for sin and for the attitude they take toward

his grace. To reject this grace serves to compound sin and guilt unto final condemnation. To enter into grace through faith in Christ enables God to put down to one's account *righteousness,* and in this righteousness is peace. Apart from grace there is no "peace with God" (5:1). Therefore, the order is not accidental when Paul says, "Grace to you and peace from God our Father, and the Lord Jesus Christ" (Rom. 1:7).

6

The Problem of Mastery

Romans 6:1–23

Justification by faith is a work of God's grace. Since it is unrelated to law or man's works, its abiding nature does not rest in the believer but in the one in whom he believes (see 2 Tim. 1:12). Man changes from moment to moment, but Jesus Christ is the same yesterday, today, and forever (see Heb. 13:8). While salvation is by grace through faith, not out of man or his works as the source, it is *unto* or should result in good works which God has before ordained that the believer should walk in or order his manner of life in (see Eph. 2:8–10). Grace is a gift, but it makes its demands upon the one receiving it.

Chapters 1–4 dealt primarily with God's righteousness, or *justification*. Chapter 5 treated the matter of sin and grace. Chapters 6–7 are related to *sanctification*. Chapter 8 deals more with *glorification* which grows out of the other two phases of salvation.

The moment one is *justified* he is *sanctified* or set apart as an instrument for God's service. Thus immediately he is confronted with the question as to who shall be the master of his life. Will it be Satan or God? Will the Christian continue to be dominated by Satan through the sin principle? Or will he be dominated by God in Christ in living according to the righteousness which he has in Christ? The answer to these questions determines whether or not the Christian will live victoriously or be defeated in the reason for his being as a Christian.

Once you receive Christ as your Savior, Satan has lost your soul forever. He then attacks you in the area of your Christian life. If he succeeds, he will not only harm or destroy your usefulness as a Christian but will largely destroy the joy that you have as a child of God. The fullness of your Christian life calls for complete surrender to God in Christ, as by the Holy Spirit you develop in knowledge and service for the Lord (see 2 Pet. 3:18). So Paul now turns to the question of mastery in Christian living.

The Question of Sin and Grace (6:1-2)

At this point in Romans Paul returns to his debate with an imaginary Jewish questioner. This debate reflects a synagogue setting.

In his previous argument Paul has shown that legalism has no part in God's redemptive purpose other than to convict man of sin. To the contrary he has avowed that salvation is by grace through faith. In 3:8 Paul alluded to the charge made by the legalists that his gospel of grace was an encouragement for men to sin. Now he takes up this charge, directing his argument toward the antinomians or those who lived in sin as if there were no law against it. They completely misunderstood what is involved in God's grace. Rather than to see it as calling for gratitude to God and complete devotion to his will, they regarded it as a license to live in sin.

"What shall we say then? Shall we continue in sin, that grace may abound?" (v. 1). These are rhetorical questions which Paul uses to introduce his refutation of such an idea. These questions actually did not originate with Paul but were being asked by the legalists and the antinomians. They evidently had reference to the apostle's words in 5:20. If it be true that where sin abounds grace superabounds with more grace beyond that, then the way to have more grace is to have more sin. Implied is the idea that sinners were actually serving God in sinning by giving him the opportunity to demonstrate his grace.

"Continue" is the translation of a Greek verb meaning to abide upon. In 1 Corinthians 16:8 Paul used it of tarrying in Ephesus. The present tense means to have the habit of continuing to live in sin. In the Greek, both "sin" and "grace" have the definite article, as in 5:20. "The grace," of course, means the grace which God shows to sinners. "The sin" apparently refers to the sin principle or one's sinful nature. But, of course, this sinful nature expresses itself in *sins*. One who is mastered by the sin principle will give evidence of that fact by having the habit of sinning; so in the final analysis *sins* as well as the sinful nature are involved.

"God forbid. How shall we that are dead to sin, live any longer therein?" (v. 2). Here again is Paul's vehement refusal of such an idea (see 3:4, 6, 31). Let not such an idea come into being. "By no means!" (RSV). No! No! Perish the thought! Then he gives his reason for so emphatic a rejection. When we (Jews and Gentiles) received Christ as Savior, we died to the sinful nature. A dead man cannot be tempted by the allurements of evil. How shall such a dead man continue to be dominated by his sinful nature?

Let us suppose that a man whose weakness is alcohol dies. While he lived, the very smell of it set his appetite for it aflame, but after his death you can wave an open bottle of it under his nose and he will give no reaction. In like fashion one who has died to his sinful nature is in his spiritual self immune to sin's enticements. So human logic itself denies the idea that a truly regenerated person will have the habit of living under the domination of sin.

No purely human picture fully illustrates spiritual truth. It is true that on occasion, so long as the Christian abides in a fleshly body, he may in a moment of weakness slip and fall into a given sin. However, he repents, asking God's forgiveness and asking for strength not to sin. Nevertheless, the New Testament never promises sinless perfection in this life. Those who claim to have achieved it are victims of the ancient Gnostic dualism which distinguished between the flesh and the spirit.

The New Testament does not teach that the body is inherently evil (see 1 Cor. 6:19–20) or that deeds of the flesh do not affect the spirit. Some see certain verses in 1 John as teaching that a Christian does not sin (see 3:6, 9), but in the Greek text the meaning is that such do not make sinning the habit of their lives ("sinneth," v. 6, and "commit" or "do," v. 9, both are present tenses). Furthermore, 1 John was written to Christians (note "my little children," 2:1). First John 1:10 should read, "never at any time sinned" (aorist tense). Also 1 John 1:9 may read, "If we from time to time [when we sin] confess our sins, he is continuously faithful and just in order that he may forgive us from time to time [when we confess], our sins and cleanse us from all unrighteousness" (the present tense in certain contexts may read "from time to time").

However, this is a far cry from the situation with which Paul is dealing in Romans 6:1–2. It involves the idea of whether a Christian may make sinning the habit of his life. This he strongly denies.

The Meaning of Baptism (6:3–5)

Paul illustrates the idea of Christians dying to sin by pointing to the meaning depicted in the act of baptism. To see these verses as teaching that baptism is necessary for salvation is to inject an idea foreign to Paul's theology. In no sense was he a sacramentarian. These words were written within the context of justification by grace through faith.

"Know ye not, that so many of us as were baptized into Jesus Christ [Christ Jesus] were baptized into his death?" (v. 3). The word *baptized,* of course, is not a translation but a transliteration of the Greek word *baptizō.* A translation would read "immerse." The word means to dip, plunge, submerge, immerse. It is used in nonbiblical Greek of a ship sinking. There was a time when one might need to dwell at length upon this matter, but no more. Scholarship is agreed that the word means to immerse, regardless of a departure from it in practice by many. No Baptist has written a Greek lexicon; yet all lexicons with which I am familiar give the meaning of *baptizō* as immerse. Moody says, "A modern scholar arguing for any mode other than immersion on biblical and historical grounds is hard pressed for evidence. This is not a Baptist prejudice. Catholic comments run much the same as Protestants, for Joseph A. Fitzmyer, cautiously says: 'Paul's discussion here is most easily understood of baptism by immersion' (IBC)" (p. 198). For a full discussion of this see Robertson's article on "Baptism" in *The International Standard Bible Encyclopaedia* (James Orr, ed., 5 vols., rev. ed. [Grand Rapids, Mich., Wm. B. Eerdmans, 1930]).

Actually Christian baptism is immersion in water and emersion from water. Immersion alone is drowning. It depicts only a dying and burial. Emersion depicts a resurrection.

"Know ye not" assumes that Paul's readers do know. The basic form of the gospel is "Christ died . . . was buried . . . he rose again" (1 Cor. 15:3–4). The apostle assumes that they know these rudimentary elements of gospel truth as it related to Christian baptism.

The key word in verses 3–4 is "into" (*eis,* see Acts 2:38). Does it mean that in baptism the believer enters into Christ? No more so than "buried with him by baptism" means that we enter into death (see v. 4). The preposition *eis* may be translated variously: into, unto, for, at (see Matt. 12:41), as the result of, with reference to. It seems that the last meaning applies here. Thus "so many of us as were baptized with reference to Christ Jesus, with reference to his death were baptized."

This same thought continues in verse 4: "Therefore, we were buried with him through the baptism with reference to the death, in order that like as Christ was raised out of the realm of the dead through the glory of the Father, even so also in newness of life we may walk" (literal). "In order that" (*hina*) introduces a purpose clause. The purpose being that in sharing in Christ's new life following his resurrection, we also shall walk or order our new lives in keeping with the continuing life of Christ. "The glory of the Father" refers to his power exhibited

in the bodily resurrection of Christ. This power also imparts
new life to the believer. It guarantees our own resurrection
through his Spirit who indwells us (see 8:11).

Note that Christian baptism depicts both a burial (implying
death) and a resurrection. The word translated "baptism" is
baptismatos, a form of *baptisma*. *Baptismos* connotes the act of
baptism. It is never used in the New Testament for Christian
baptism. The word so used here is *baptisma* which means the
meaning in the act. It is not found outside the New Testament
except in subsequent ecclesiastical writings.

This word is especially significant in this passage (see also
1 Pet. 3:21). Baptism itself does not contribute to salvation. It
connotes the experience which has already happened. Actually
it symbolizes what Jesus Christ did for our salvation: death,
burial, and resurrection. It also symbolizes that which Christ
through the Holy Spirit does in the believer: he dies to his old
sinful nature; it is buried; and the Christian is raised to a new
life in Christ. It also pictures one's faith in the final bodily
resurrection (v. 5). However, the primary thought here is the
death to the sinful nature and the rising to a new manner of
life and mastery in Christ. To confuse the picture with the reality is to lose the meaning involved in both.

The Dying and Living with Christ (6:6–11)

Paul continues to show that his readers, by virtue of their
Christian experience, have died to the control of their sinful nature. The result is that they should live with and for Christ,
however, from the figure of baptism he moves to the cross and
shows how both Christ and the believer died/dies.

"Knowing" (v. 6) is knowing from experience. Paul assumes
that each of his readers has had the experience of dying and
living with Christ. "Our old man" refers to the unregenerated
man. The Greek word for "man" (*anthropos*) is the generic
term for man or mankind. The word for a male person is *anēr*.
Anthropos, therefore, can refer to both male and female in this
context, or to every single person. The Greek language had two
words for "old." *Archaios* means old with respect to time, but
the word here, *palaios*, means old with respect to use. It is something worn out and fit only to be discarded. In Colossians 3:9
Paul uses the "old man" in terms of old, worn-out clothes (see
Eph. 4:22).

"Our old man is crucified." In Galatians 2:20 Paul says, "I
am crucified with Christ." He so identified himself with Christ's
death as to see himself on the cross with him. This is the sense

here. Of course, Christ died for all men, but for his death to avail for one man, the man must identify himself with Christ through a personal faith in him. "The body of sin" connotes the body before justification, a body under the control of the sinful nature. "Might be destroyed" is the translation of a Greek verb which means to render idle or inoperative, to make inactive, or to cause to cease. Since the body of flesh remains after regeneration, perhaps the best sense here is "to render inactive or inoperative." This does not mean that the sinful nature does not continue to assert itself (see chap. 7). Being rendered inoperative is explained in the words "that henceforth [no longer] we should not serve sin" or "the sinful nature."

"Serve" is the translation of a present infinitive meaning to keep on serving as a slave or to do so as a habit of life. To be a slave means to give absolute loyalty to one's owner. Jesus used this same infinitive twice in Matthew 6:24: "No one is able to be a slave to two owners. . . . It is not possible to be a slave to God and to mammon." Each demands absolute loyalty and service, which you cannot provide for two different owners. In Romans 6:6 Paul is saying that formerly his readers' bodies belonged to Satan or to the sinful nature, and they had the habit of serving such. Now they have a new *owner;* so they should no longer habitually serve their former owner. A new relationship calls for a new allegiance.

"For he that is dead is freed from sin" (v. 7), actually, "is fully justified [perfect tense] away from the sinful nature." One may from time to time yield to it, but he is not obligated to make sin the habit of his life. Indeed, through the indwelling of the Holy Spirit (see John 14:16–18) Christ furnishes the power by which to overcome the overtures of the sinful nature. It is in this sense that the Christian is liberated from the tyranny of the sinful nature. Here Paul clearly introduces the idea of a choice of masters in the Christian's life, a matter which he discusses more fully beginning with verse 12.

"If we be dead with Christ" (v. 8) assumes that this is true. Since that is the case, we keep on believing that we shall also live with him. The Greek verb translated "shall live" denotes spiritual life. "With Christ" may also read "with respect to Christ" or by means of the spiritual life which he gives. It is not a temporary but an eternal life. It is the quality of life which the Christian has here and now and which abides in eternity. This idea is reflected in "completely justified" in verse 7.

This truth is emphasized in verses 9–10. "Knowing" expresses perceptive knowledge or soul conviction. The believer knows without question that Christ, being raised from the dead, dies no more. Death no longer "exercises dominion" over him. The verb so translated comes from the word for lord or owner (*kurios*). Death no longer lords it over Christ. It had him in its clutches once for three short days—but never again. Instead, Christ is Lord over death. In his death with respect to sin, he died "once for all" (*ephapax*, see Heb. 9:26–28). Having died and risen again, "he keeps on living with respect to God" (literal).

In verse 11 Paul draws a conclusion based upon Christ's experience: "Likewise . . . ye also." "Ye" is emphatic, setting the Christian's experience in a proper relationship to that of Christ. As Christ died for sin once for all and now continues to live with respect to God, so also the Christian should "reckon," or enter into the ledger of his conduct, himself to be dead to the sinful nature but living spiritually with respect to God. This he does "in the sphere of Christ Jesus." The phrase "our Lord" is not found in the best texts.

It should be recalled that in chapters 6 and 7 Paul is discussing sanctification. The very second that one believes in Jesus Christ he is justified or declared just before God. He dies to his old sinful nature to be made alive unto God. At the same time he is sanctified or set apart as an instrument for God's service. Thereafter, he is to grow, develop, and serve in the state of sanctification. He runs down the flag of allegiance or slavery to his sinful nature and runs up the flag of allegiance and slavery to God in Christ. Being dead to the power of his sinful nature, he should no longer serve it. Being in Christ and Christ being in him, he does not have to serve sin. If he does so, he does it of his own free will, but in the process he betrays him to whom he has sworn a new allegiance. The best positive answer to the sinful nature is to serve God aggressively. You can do this "in the sphere of Christ Jesus."

A Christian is no longer a "natural" or unredeemed person (see 1 Cor. 2:14), but he faces the danger of being a "carnal" Christian or one controlled by his fleshly appetites (see 1 Cor. 3:1). His only alternative is to be a "spiritual" or Spirit-controlled Christian (see 1 Cor. 3:1). This is God's intended purpose for every one of his children who is in the state of justification and sanctification.

The Call to Christian Commitment (6:12–14)

At this point Paul comes to grips with the question of mastery in the Christian's life. Thus far in chapter 6 he has laid the theological grounds for the subject. Now he calls for action in the light of it. On the basis that the Christian is dead to his sinful nature and alive to God, Paul exhorts his readers to realize the full potential of their sanctification experience.

"Let not sin therefore reign in your mortal body, that ye should obey it in the lusts thereof" (v. 12). The Christian must recognize that he can say no to the evil desires which clamor for expression in his body. The power to do this is available through God's indwelling Spirit.

"Therefore" refers to verses 1–11. "Mortal body" means one that is subject to death. "Lusts" is a translation of the Greek word meaning "desires." They may be good or evil desires. In relation to sin they become lusts. The desires are legitimate, but to express them under the reign of evil perverts them into lusts. "Obey" is a present infinitive meaning to hear under or in submission. The present tense means to have the habit of doing so. This is not permission for an occasional lapse into sin, but it forbids the Christian from making this his life-style.

More specifically in verse 13 the apostle adds that the Christian should not yield or place alongside the parts of his body as "instruments" of unrighteousness unto the sinful nature. "Instruments" translates a word (*hopla*) used for tools or for weapons for warfare. "Tools" fits the idea of slavery. One should not use the parts of his body as tools with which to serve his sinful nature. Seen as "weapons," this suggests the Christian as a soldier, a term often used by Paul. Various translations differ as to whether these are "tools" or "weapons," but the context seems to favor the latter. The sinful nature continues to try to reign in the Christian's life. He is to reject this, and he is not to use his body's members as weapons fighting for unrighteousness against righteousness, or for Satan in his warfare against God.

On the contrary, Christians are to "yield themselves" or place themselves on the side of God. He has made them alive from the dead; so they should place their members as weapons of righteousness to fight on God's side. One cannot have a divided allegiance. He cannot fight on one side or the other as he chooses. One wearing the armor of righteousness should not be found fighting in the ranks of unrighteousness. In his former state of unrighteousness the Christian gave full allegiance to Satan. Now he must as zealously give it to God. Alas, how many who have sworn allegiance to Christ take it so lightly! If you *are* a Christian, you should *be* a Christian with undivided loyalty toward God.

"For sin [without the definite article] shall not have dominion [mastery] over you" (v. 14). Sin shall not lord it over the

Christian. Even though sin is not completely dead, it shall not
be the controlling factor in the Christian's life since "ye are not
under the law, but under grace." In the Greek text "law" has
no definite article. Here Paul returns to the question of the
relation of law to grace (see 6:1). Rather than encouraging one
to sin, his gospel is precisely the reason why the Christian
should not sin. One's gratitude for God's grace should serve as
a deterrent to sin. It should lead to total commitment to God.
One who has been liberated from legalism and the tyranny of
sin should be all the more devoted to God who liberated him.
Willingness to give the mastery in one's life to that which de-
stroys is folly indeed. Sane reckoning (see v. 11) of the alter-
natives will lead one to yield gladly to the benevolent rule of
God in one's life.

The Question of Loyalty (6:15–23)

It is evident that seated deep in Paul's consciousness is the
relation of law to the tyranny of sin. Moody (p. 202) reminds us
that "law is also lord where sin has dominion, for it functions
to arouse the awareness of sin (3:20), to work the wrath of God
by making sin a trespass of the law (4:15), and actually increasing the sovereignty of sin (5:20)." So Paul closes this
chapter with a strong appeal for loyalty to God rather than to
sin.

"What then? shall we sin, because we are not under the law,
but under grace? God forbid" (v. 15). "What then" is Paul's
device in debate with his imaginary Jewish questioner. He injects the charge that grace encourages sin, while law discour-
ages it, into the appeal for God's mastery in the Christian's life.
The apostle also narrows the scope of the argument from continuing in "the sin" or sinful nature (see 6:1) to an occasional
sin. This latter picture is seen in the aorist tense of the verb in
"shall we sin" (v. 15). "Law" here in the Greek has no definite
article, so it means legalism. This point of attack touches us
all. It is so easy to excuse sinning occasionally on the basis that
we are not under law but under grace. However, Paul rejects
this idea as strongly as he does that of continuing habitually
to live in the sinful nature. "God forbid!"

Verse 16 gives the reason. Returning to the idea of slavery,
Paul asks, "Know ye not?" or "do you not really know?"—perceptive knowledge. Do you not know what? For one thing, that
men's lives are made up of loyalty or obedience—whether to the
bad or to the good. In this sense all men are slaves to someone
or something. For another thing, that to which you give your

loyalty is your master and you are its slave. In this sense, you are either a slave to Satan or to God. He who commits sin is a slave to sin, said Jesus (see John 8:34). Likewise, he who serves God is a slave to God. In becoming a Christian one is freed from the tyrannical slavery to Satan to submit to the benevolent slavery to God (see Col. 1:13).

I sat one day in a courtroom and witnessed the ceremony in which aliens became citizens of the United States. The final act before their becoming citizens was to renounce allegiance to their former nation and to swear allegiance to the United States, including their oath to bear arms and to defend their new nation against any foreign aggression even if the aggressor should be their former nation. This is what is involved in becoming a citizen of God's kingdom.

Paul expresses this in the remainder of verse 16. One is a slave to whomever he gives his allegiance to obey—"whether of sin unto death, or of obedience [to God] unto righteousness." "Sin" is without the definite article, so a sinful act. Robertson (p. 364) comments, "As Paul used the figure to illustrate death to sin and resurrection to new life in Christ and not in sin, so now he uses slavery against the idea of occasional lapses into sin. Loyalty to Christ will not permit occasional crossing over to the other side to Satan's line." Wuest (p. 109) speaks of the impossibility of a believer living a life of "planned occasional sin." This suggests the medieval abuse of "indulgences" by the Roman Catholic church. One might purchase an indulgence granting forgiveness for a past sin or for a sin one planned to commit in the future. "Planned occasional sin" suggests that one is not a Christian but is still under the tyranny of his sinful nature. A Christian may/will sin on occasion, but he does not plan to do so in advance. The difference is that between killing in a fit of anger and deliberate premeditated murder.

"But God be thanked" (v. 17). Paul does not thank God that his readers were the slaves of sin. He is grateful that they obeyed out of the heart (seat of the will or total inner person) the form of teaching which was "delivered" to them in the gospel. The result was that being liberated from "the sin" (sinful nature) they became slaves "to the righteousness" of God (v. 18). "Delivered" in verse 17 translates a verb meaning to give alongside. It was used of handing over Jesus for crucifixion, but here the figure is used of the slave market. The seller of a slave delivered him to the buyer, but "out of the heart" means that under the new standard of righteousness through grace declared in the gospel, a slave to the sinful nature by his own consent was handed over to God, his new master or owner.

Because of the weakness of his readers' flesh, or inability to
grasp spiritual truth, Paul says that he is speaking "after the
manner of men" (v. 19). Evidently this is an apology for using
the figure of slavery along with that of righteousness. Nevertheless, it is a good figure drawn from the social order of the
day to express spiritual truth. In time past men had yielded
their bodies to "uncleanness and to iniquity unto iniquity." "Iniquity" is the translation of the Greek word for "lawlessness."
Impure living was rampant in pagan life (see 1:21–32). Lawlessness increased into more lawlessness. Charles B. Williams
translates this phrase "to ever increasing lawlessness." But now
they have been regenerated: "So now yield your members slaves
to righteousness unto holiness" (literal).

Paul's pre-Christian and Christian life is a commentary on
this verse. Before becoming a Christian he used all his powers
to fight against Christ. As a Christian he dedicated them to fighting on the side of Christ.

"Holiness" should read "sanctification." The Greek word is
hagiasmos which connotes progressive sanctification. The word
for the finished process is *hagiōsunē* (see 1 Thess. 3:13). This
does not negate the idea of the believer's being sanctified or set
apart to God's service simultaneously with regeneration (see
"saints" or "holy ones," 1 Cor. 1:2). In the state of being sanctified the Christian should progressively grow in sanctification,
looking toward the finished work in heaven. As slaves of their
sinful nature, men were "free" with respect to righteousness.
They had no righteousness either in personal conduct or in
standing before God (v. 20). The apostle rightly asks what
fruit they had from such. They had only shame concerning
their previous conduct (v. 21). "But now" they were "free"
from the sinful nature. Free from that slavery, they now are
slaves to God, and this slavery produces fruit unto "holiness"
or progressive growth in progressively overcoming sin in their
state of sanctification. The end or goal of this is life eternal.
This does not mean that one will not know whether he is saved
until the end of the age. "Eternal life" is the quality of life
which one has now and which abides in eternity. However, the
idea here is the consummation of righteous living in a per-
fected sanctification which results in glorification.

"For the wages of [the] sin is death; but the gift of God is
eternal life through Jesus Christ our Lord" (v. 23). "The sin,"
of course, refers to the sinful nature. "Wages" refers to a Greek
soldier's pay, either in cash or rations. Satan pays his soldiers
their wages—death. God's free gift (*charisma*, the product of
his grace), not earned wages, is age-abiding life. It is not due to

any works of man but is provided in the sphere of (*en*) the redemptive work of "Christ Jesus our Lord."

Thus Paul has presented the two possible masteries—Satan and God. If one never gives himself to God in Christ, death, spoken of here in the spiritual sense, is his pay from his satanic master. A Christian may be a carnal one—his soul is saved but his Christian life is lost (see 1 Cor. 3:11–15)—but the one who would be saved in both soul and Christian life should choose the mastery of God. Only thus may he have the abundant and overflowing life which Christ came to give (see John 10:10).

7

The Conflict of Desires

Romans 7:1–25

Romans 7 is actually a continuation of the thought in Romans 6. Even as Paul exhorts his readers to make God the master of their Christian lives, he recognizes that this is not as simple as it may seem, and he is frank and kind enough to use his own experience as an example of this fact. Even though he has died to his sinful nature and has been made alive in Christ, the sinful nature remains, and continues to seek to dominate through the appetites of his flesh. There is a continuous conflict between Paul's sinful nature and his new nature in Christ. It is a conflict of desires.

Paul has shown previously that the sinful nature seeks to express itself through a perversion of the benevolent intent of the law. So before baring his own soul in the matter, he reasons concerning the law and man's relation to it (vv. 1–12). Then he reveals his own personal struggle (vv. 13–23) and reaches a rousing climax of the whole (vv. 24–25).

The Analogy of Marriage and Death (7:1–6)

Paul might have used any one of a number of legal situations to illustrate his point, but he chose marriage. His thesis is the accepted fact that death cancels all contracts. But before he finishes a rather involved discussion, it becomes clear how fitting is his choice of a legal example.

He begins with a reminder to his readers that they are familiar with legal matters (v. 1). He addresses them twice as "brethren" (vv. 1, 4), a salutation not found since 1:13. Since the first use of the word, Paul has followed impassioned logic. One wonders if the sudden dual use of it here is due to the personal nature of this chapter. He reminds them that he is speaking to those who are familiar with "law" or the principle of law. Some see this as a reference to Roman law, and others regard it as denoting the Mosaic law. The absence of the definite article in the Greek leaves it as an open question. However, "law" could include both. Certainly a congregation in Rome would be familiar with Roman civil law. But there is no reason to doubt that they were familiar with the Hebrew Scriptures. Certainly those such as Aquila and Priscilla had taught them to Gentile Christians (see Acts 18:26). In any case the principle laid down by Paul applies.

"The law hath dominion over a man as long as he liveth." The definite article here clearly refers to the Mosaic law, but it is also true of any law. Only death releases a person from the authority of the law which is given to regulate human conduct. A man may be accused of a crime and be slated to stand trial. If in the meantime he dies, the case is closed. Law, other than God's law concerning salvation, does not reach beyond the grave. If civil damages are involved, the law may exact satisfaction from the estate of the deceased, but it does not touch him personally.

To illustrate his thought, Paul selects the law concerning marriage. "The woman which hath an husband is bound by the law to her husband so long as he liveth" (v. 2). "Which hath an husband" translates one word *hupandros* meaning "under a man" or in subjection to a man. Under Hebrew law a wife was regarded as her husband's property (see Exod. 20:17; Deut. 5:21). Even a married slave was not to be separated from his wife (see Exod. 21:2–3). This is seen in the perfect tense of "bound." She is bound and stands bound; so there is no release. Jesus said that Moses' law about a bill of divorcement (see Deut. 24:1–2) was due to the hardness of men's hearts (see Matt. 19:8). Since husbands were ignoring the basic law by sending their wives away, Moses commanded that wives be given a paper renouncing all legal claim to her as property so she might marry another. But Paul is thinking of the basic law.

However, if the husband died, the wife was "loosed [released] from the law of her husband." "Released" translates the Greek verb meaning to render inoperative. The law which bound the wife to her husband became inoperative. The rabbis taught that death ends all legal obligations (see Ps. 88:5); so Paul's word was in that vein.

In verse 3 he says that a woman is an adulteress if she marries another while her husband still lives. But if he is dead, she is not guilty of adultery should she remarry. It should be noted that Paul is dealing with the purely legal aspects of the matter. Jesus lifted the situation to a higher level when he said, "Except it be for fornication" (Matt. 19:9; see also Matt. 5:32). Some interpreters hold that the exception clause is not Jesus' words, but the manuscript evidence is strong for it in both instances in Matthew. The fact that Mark 10:11–12 omits it in his parallel account is cited against Matthew's record. However, close examination shows that they are not exact parallels. Jesus' words in Matthew were directed to the Pharisees who asked about divorce "for every cause" (19:3). Mark's words were spoken to the disciples later when Jesus laid down the divine ideal (see Mark 10:10).

It should be kept in mind that Paul is not dealing with specifics but with the basic Mosaic code, in which he omits even Deuteronomy 24:1–2. We must let Paul say what he says in making his particular point with regard to the Christian's relation to the law. His analogy did not call for exceptions in the real lesson he is giving.

"Wherefore" (v. 4) introduces a conclusion drawn from Paul's example. "Ye" is emphatic in the Greek text, relating his brethren's case to the law of marriage. "Ye also are become dead to the law by the body of Christ; that ye should be married to another, even to him who is raised from the dead, that we should bring forth fruit unto God."

Some see a problem at this point. In Paul's example, it is the husband who dies, but in his application it is the *wife* (the Christian brethren) who becomes dead to the Mosaic law. The analogy calls for the death of law, but Paul does not say that, for the law still exists (see Robertson, p. 366). However, Paul often mixed his figures of speech. He does so here in order to make his point that death ends the marriage bond. Having made that point, he applies it to fit his major thought, namely, that the Christian died to the law and is no longer bound by it.

Note is also taken of the verb form used to express the kind of death involved. Had the apostle been thinking only of death, he could have used the simple verb meaning "you died" (*apethanete*). Instead, he used the form of this verb which reads, "Ye were made dead" (*ethanatōthēte*), denoting a violent death. This was the kind of death Jesus died, and "through the body of Christ" the believer died the same death. Christ's death became the believer's when he believed in Christ. The believer died to end the reign of the law. In his corresponding death, the believer is liberated from death's reign over him.

"That" is the translation of *eis* followed by an infinitive, literally, "in order for you to become [married] to another." The figure corresponds to that of a wife being married to another husband. "Another" means another of a different kind. In this case the new *husband* is Christ. Contrary to law, Christ is God's means of grace. So as in chapter 6 the believer died to the slavery of sin (v. 2) to become a slave of God, so here he died to law to become married to Christ through whom God mediates his grace to man. Mixing his figures again Paul shows that Christ, the new husband, died but was raised from the dead. He arose to die no more; so this is a permanent marriage (see Gal. 2:19–20). This spiritual marriage corresponds to one in the Old Testament of God as the husband and Israel as the wife (see Jer. 2:2; Hos. 1–3). Unfaithfulness to God was pictured as spiritual adultery. May not unfaithfulness to Christ on the part of a Christian be considered the same? In Ephesians 5:22–33 Paul likens the husband-wife relationship to the Christ-church relationship.

"That" (*hina*) introduces a result clause. The result is that in the Christ-Christian marriage relationship the Christian "should bring forth fruit unto God." In 6:22 Paul spoke of "your fruit unto holiness." Here he does not specify the nature of the fruit. Robertson (p. 367) says that Paul changed the metaphor to that of a tree as in 6:22. Possibly so, but in the context of marriage this may also suggest the wife bearing children. The fruit of one Christian is another Christian.

However, in verses 5–6 the apostle contrasts the fruit of pagan living with that of Christian living. "In the flesh" (v. 5) does not mean that the flesh is inherently evil. It is subject to being dominated by evil. Paul often used *flesh* to denote life apart from God. *The Twentieth Century New Testament* reads, "When we were living merely earthly lives." "The motions of sin" should read "the passions [*pathēmata*] of sin" or passions marked by sin. Moffatt renders this "sinful cravings." These were "through the law," and they energized or began and continued working in themselves (imperfect middle) in our bodily members, the result being to produce the fruit of death. "Death" here refers to spiritual death or the soul's separation from God. The imperfect form of the verb shows the continuing absolute control of the sinful nature over the unbelieving person.

"But now" (v. 6) contrasts the saved condition with the unsaved state. What is the new condition? The Christian has been discharged from bondage to the law. He is dead to that which held him in bondage. "So that we should serve in newness of spirit, and not in the oldness of the letter." This is the purpose of the new life in Christ.

"Serve" means to serve as a slave. Thus Paul again takes up the idea of mastery discussed in chapter 6. "Newness" is contrasted with "oldness." The former means new, not in time, but in quality. It is in contrast to the oldness of that which is worn out from use and needs to be discarded. "Letter" (*gramma*) is that which has been written. Here it refers to the Mosaic code as written in the Hebrew Scriptures. Does "spirit" refer to the human spirit or to the Holy Spirit? The logical sense calls for the latter. Now God deals with man through the Holy Spirit, as formerly he dealt through the written law. The Holy Spirit creates this newness of life, that which the law could not do. This verse further suggests that the Holy Spirit gives power by which to live according to God's will (see 8:2). The law said, "Do this," but it had no power to help one to obey the command. As the Christian faces the conflict of desires in him, he has an ally to enable him to be victorious over evil.

The Purpose of Law (7:7–13)

At this point we come to a new section of the subject under consideration. From here to the end of the chapter Paul relates the nature of the law to human conduct. Is this section autobiographical or is Paul describing the experience of every man? Moody (p. 207) quotes T. W. Manson: "Here Paul's autobiography is the biography of every man." The lavish use of the personal pronoun *I* strongly suggests that the apostle is relating his own experience, but what he says of himself is also true of all others who have walked the same path.

A further question is raised: Does Romans 7:7–24 relate to Paul's preconversion or postconversion experience? This question is asked especially regarding verses 13–24. A strong list of scholars can be cited for both positions. Wuest (p. 118) suggests that the entire section relates to Paul's and other Christians' experiences, when, as Christians, they put themselves under the law (vv. 7–13) and when they learn to rely upon Christ alone (vv. 14–25). "In 7:7–13, he [Paul] shows that a believer putting himself under law, thus failing to avail himself of the resources of grace, is a defeated Christian (here he recounts his own experience as a Christian before he came to the knowledge of Romans 6); and in 7:14–25, he teaches that while the law incites this Christian to more sin, yet the law is not responsible for that sin, but his evil nature, which only can be conquered as the believer cries, 'Who shall deliver me?' and thus looks away from himself and self-dependence to the Lord Jesus." This difference in attitude could be reflected in the repeated use of the aorist (past) tense in verses 7–14 and the use of the present tense, with very few exceptions (one aorist, two perfects, and one future), in verses 14–25.

However, it is this use of tenses which leads me to see verses 7–13 as referring to Paul's preconversion experience and verses 14–25 as related to the struggle within his life as a Christian. And, of course, as Manson says, while autobiographical, it is

also the biography of every person who turns from unbelief to
faith in Jesus Christ. Much may be said for the other positions,
but one must choose.

In this light, therefore, Paul raises or anticipates a question
from his imaginary Jewish questioner. Having shown that the
Christian has died to the law to be wedded to Christ, one might
well wonder if Paul is downgrading the law. "Is the law sin?"
(v. 7). Again, his "God forbid" strongly rejects such an idea.
It was "law" (no definite article) which led him to know sin
by experience. As an example Paul uses the commandment
"Thou shalt not covet." Except for this law he would not have
really known that it was a sin to covet. Both "lust" and "covet"
translate the Greek word for desire, but in the evil sense. William F. Beck (*The New Testament in the Language of Today*)
translates it, "For example, only when the Law said, Don't lust,
did I know how wrong it is to lust." Thus Paul's sinful nature,
or tendency toward sin, taking this as "occasion" or a starting
place, worked in him every single kind (*pasan*) of evil desire.
Because apart from law sin was dead. This does not mean that
evil desire was not sin before the law forbade it but that the
law brought to Paul the experiential and soul knowledge that
evil desire was sin. The very fact that the law forbade it in-
flamed his sinful nature to do it. Forbidden fruit is always the
sweetest to unregenerated human nature.

Continuing, he says that once he was "alive" apart from
law, but when the commandment came, sin revived and he
was "dead." "Alive" probably means that until he knew the
commandment he had evil desire without a sense of guilt—
such as a child in the age of innocence—but when he knew the
law forbidding it, the sense of sin recovered its vigor or expressed itself. No longer could he sin in blissful ignorance.
He was "dead" to any lack of guilt. Ignorance is no excuse under law, but it does give one a sense of guiltlessness at the
time.

Suppose that I am driving my car in a strange city. Innocently I turn to go the wrong way on a one-way street. Even
though I am ignorant about the law, my ignorance may result
in a serious accident and/or death. In my heart, however, I am
innocent of breaking the law. But once I see a sign "One Way"
pointing in the opposite direction, I become conscious of breaking the law. To persist in breaking it only compounds the evil
I am doing.

In like manner, even though he was ignorant of the fact,
Paul in his unredeemed state was violating God's law. He was,
therefore, dead spiritually. The aorist tense points to the his-

torical moment when he "died," that is, that he knew he was
dead spiritually. The commandment which was meant for life
was found by Paul to be unto death (v. 10). It was good in its
purpose, but "the sinful nature," seizing the opportunity through
the commandment, deceived him and slew him (v. 11). The
verb translated "slew" means to kill off, to make a complete
job of it.

Paul concludes, therefore, that the law is "holy" (v. 12). This
means that it is from "a sphere other than this world. The law
is divine and has in it the very voice of God" (Barclay, p. 94).
The commandment is *just* (settling aright all human and divine relationships); and it is *good* (designed for the highest
good for the greatest number of people).

So Paul again raises a question (v. 13): Did this good law
become death for him? Again, he strongly rejects such an idea.
God forbid! It was his sinful nature which was working death
through the good, so that it might appear as sin. The holy, just,
and good law of God took its toll through Paul's violation of it.
It was to the end that his sinful nature might in violation of
God's law become "exceeding sinful." "Exceeding" is the translation of a Greek word meaning a casting beyond (*huperbolēn*,
note *hyperbole*). Denney says, "Sin turns God's intended blessing into a curse; nothing could more clearly show what it is,
or excite a stronger desire for deliverance from it" (pp. 640–
41). Robertson adds, "The excesses of sin reveal its real nature.
Only then do some people get their eyes opened" (p. 369).

So Paul justifies the nature of the law. To the casual observer
it might appear to be bad, but through careful analysis the
apostle shows that, despite Satan's efforts to abuse the law, the
result is to reveal sin for what it is. It promises life but delivers
death. It offers happiness but produces sorrow. It speaks of a
full realization of life but leads to despair. One cannot help
but see in Paul's preconversion experience a reenactment of the
tragedy described in Genesis 3. Even so, when one has run the
full course of sin's allurements, he is ready to turn to him who
saves from sin. Saul of Tarsus learned that as good as the law
is it does not satisfy the deepest longings of the soul. He found
that in Jesus one noonday on the Damascus road.

The Inward Warfare (7:14–23)

If my stated position is right in regard to Romans 7:7–25,
then the division in Paul's experience comes between verses
13 and 14. Verse 14 contains the first of a long series of present
tenses, along with two perfect tenses which point to past com-

pleted action which continues into the present. Thus we conclude that verses 14–25 refer to his postconversion experience. At this point we should refer to verses 5–6. Through bitter experience Paul had to learn that, being delivered from legalism, he should serve the Lord in his new quality of life.

"For we know that the law is spiritual: but I am carnal, sold under sin" (v. 14). "Know" is a perfect tense of completeness. It expresses perceptive knowledge or a conviction of the soul. From his past experience Paul knows absolutely that the law is spiritual. The Greek word translated "spiritual" means Spirit-controlled. On the other hand, Paul says, "I am carnal." A carnal man is made of flesh. Some manuscripts read *sarkikos,* one belonging to the flesh. The stronger manuscripts read *sarkinos,* of flesh or fleshy. Denney notes that *sarkinos* means material substance, as opposed to the ethical idea in *sarkikos.* As *flesh* one is seen in his human nature rather than in his human character. "Flesh has such an exclusive preponderance that man can only be regarded as a being who has no affinity for the spiritual law of God, and necessarily kicks against it" (p. 641). Moody (p. 210) says that *sarkinos* "describes natural man, but Christians may live like natural men (1 Cor. 3:3–4)."

Note, however, that Paul does not say that he is a "natural" or unredeemed man, one controlled by the animal principle of life (see 1 Cor. 2:14). He does not claim to be a "spiritual" man or one fully controlled by the Holy Spirit (see 1 Cor. 3:1). Rather he is a "carnal" man, a carnal Christian, redeemed but still living in his fleshy body (see 1 Cor. 3:1, 3). Though a Christian, he still lives in a body of flesh with all its appetites, and his sinful nature still tries to dominate him. Nowhere does the great apostle bare his soul as to the inner struggle as he does here. If Paul had this struggle, certainly no other Christian is immune to it. The very fact that he tried to live in the will of God made the struggle all the more evident to him. The closer to God one is, the more conscious he will be of his sins.

"Sold under sin" or the sinful nature. What does Paul mean by this? Of course, those who relate this entire passage to Paul's pre-Christian state interpret this to mean complete bondage to sin. The perfect tense of "sold" supports such a meaning. However, from this point on through verse 25, with the exception of a future tense in verse 24, Paul uses the present tense. Of course, the present tense does express repeated or habitual action in the present. The imperfect tense would normally be used to express habitual action in the past and leading up to the present. The aorist or historical tense could have expressed the past fact. At times the historical present is used, but this does not seem to be the case here. The conflict described between two natures hardly allows this meaning. It seems that Paul is not describing a past but a present experience.

Weymouth translates this "I am unspiritual, sold to sin." Denney sees "sold under sin" to mean "a slave of sin." He says, "To speak of man as 'flesh' is to speak of him as distinguished from God who is 'Spirit'; but owing to the diffusion of sin in humanity, and the ascendency it has acquired, this mere distinction becomes an antagonism, and the mind of 'the flesh' is enmity against God" (p. 641).

To me, the overall picture seems to be that of a Christian living in a fleshy body, the nature of which clamors for expression in conflict with his new nature in Christ. In regeneration one is redeemed from sin's penalty but not from its power as it continues to assert its power and presence through the body of flesh. It is a struggle between the law and the spirit, the law in this case being a perversion of the spiritual intent of God's commandments. Satan endeavors to defeat the Christian's life, its growth and usefulness in the state of sanctification.

In verses 15–22 Paul describes the civil war that rages in him. "For that which I do I allow not" (v. 15). "Allow" should read "know" (*ginōskō*). Paul does not recognize or understand what is happening to him. Any person who thinks his battle with sin is over as soon as he believes in Jesus is in for a surprise. Though liberated from sin's penalty, sin continues to assert its power and presence. Indeed, the struggle intensifies as a person's new nature comes into conflict with his sinful nature. In the unredeemed life there is scarcely any struggle, for sinning is a way of life, but once a person acquires a redeemed nature in Christ, the battle is joined.

"For what I would, that do I not; but what I hate, that do I" (v. 15). "Not" is emphatic. Paul does not practice (*prassō*) what he wills or wishes to do. Instead, he does that which he hates. No unsaved person would say this. As a Christian Paul hates sin; yet he goes on doing it. "If then I do that which I would not [a condition assumed as true], I consent unto the law that it is good" (v. 16). The fact that he does not want to sin is proof as to the benevolent nature of the law. "Consent" translates a word which means to speak together with or to concur with. Since the law forbids what his redeemed nature does not want to do, his feeling concurs with the law. The word for "good" (*kalos*) refers to the moral beauty of the law. "Good" in verse 12 (*agathē*) means beneficial purpose.

"Now then it is no more I that do it, but sin that dwelleth in me" (v. 17), literally, "the indwelling in me sin." Paul is not saying that his flesh is separate from his spirit and that sin of the flesh does not affect the spirit. "I" refers to Paul's redeemed self which does not want to sin. "I" is emphatic. It is not his true self but his lower self that sins. This is because, even though his spiritual self is redeemed, sin still indwells him in the demands of his flesh. Neither does Paul claim that his true self bears no moral responsibility. His redeemed self does not control the indwelling sin; so his "I" is to that extent responsible.

Denney is helpful at this point. "To be saved from sin, a man must at the same time own it and disown it; it is this practical paradox which is reflected in this verse. It is safe for a Christian like Paul—it is not safe for everybody—to explain his failings by the watchword, Not I, but indwelling sin . . . a true saint may say it in a moment of passion, but a sinner had better not make it a principle" (pp. 641–42).

In verse 18 Paul recognizes that in his flesh dwells no good thing. He is not saying that flesh within itself is evil but that his flesh had been captivated by his sinful nature. In his true self he wills to do the good, the beautiful thing (*kalos*), but how "to work the good not" (literal reading). "To work" is an aorist infinitive. Never at any time has he found how within himself to work the good. Verses 19–20 repeat the thought of verses 15 and 17.

Out of this struggle Paul draws a conclusion. "I find then a [the] law, that, when I would do good, evil is present with me" (v. 21). The verb translated "is present" means literally "lies beside." When he lays down his will of the true self to do the good, evil lies alongside it. Someone said that if one builds a cathedral to God's glory Satan will erect a chapel beside it.

"The law" could refer to a scientific principle or to the Mosaic law, but here the context calls for another meaning. Paul is speaking of an unfailing principle that when he wills to do good, evil seeks to thwart his purpose. This law is the indwelling sin which besets him on every hand. Paul delights in the law of God according to, or within, "the inward man." The "inward man" need not mean the regenerated self although that may be the apostle's meaning here. The "inward man" is the unseen part of man's nature, his rational and moral consciousness. It is that about one which wants to do right as opposed to the outward, fleshly man which has a tendency toward sin. To "delight" is more than to "consent" (see v. 16). In fact, it may mean to "rejoice." So Paul in his inner self rejoices in God's law. Why then does he not always live according to it?

"But I see another law in my members, warring against the law of my mind, and bringing me into captivity to the law of [the] sin which is in my members" (v. 23). "Another" means another of a different kind than the law of God, which may

also be seen as the law of the mind which rejoices in the law
of God. "Warring against" translates a verb which means to
wage warfare or to carry on a military campaign against someone. It appears only here in the New Testament. This warring
succeeds in that it takes captive and enslaves the "law of my
mind," making it the slave of the law of sin in Paul's body.

"Law of my mind" corresponds to the law of the "inward
man." "Mind" to the Greeks referred to the inner man, including
the spiritual qualities of the person. Robertson notes that "ancient writers (Plato, Ovid, Seneca, Epictetus) describe the same
dual struggle in man between his conscience and his deeds"
(p. 370). Although Denney regards Paul's struggle as that of
his preconversion experience, he sees it as "the unregenerate
man's experience, surviving at least in memory into regenerate
days, and read with regenerate eyes" (p. 641). He concludes
that "Paul does not see in his nature two normal modes in
which certain forces operate; he sees two authorities saying to
him, Do this, and the higher succumbing to the lower" (p. 643).
These words are true whether one regards it as Paul's preconversion or postconversion experience. Every Christian who
seriously tries to serve the Lord can identify with this experience. On the grounds of the profuse use of the present tense,
as previously stated, I see the experience as belonging to his
postconversion life. One cannot be dogmatic, but one must make
a choice.

The Hope of Victory (7:24-25)

In desperation Paul cries for help. Unable to cope with his
problem within himself, he looks for help elsewhere.

"O wretched man that I am! who shall deliver me from the
body of this death?" (v. 24). Note that he says, "I am" not "I
was." The Greek text has no verb in this exclamation, so the
phrase reads literally, "Wretched man, I!" The Greek word
translated "wretched" is an adjective formed of the words
meaning "to carry" and "callous." Paul is wretched or bears
callouses as the result of hard labor. Exhausted in his struggle, he cries for aid.

It is logical to supply the verb in the present tense. Whether
it is the memory of a past condition or a statement of a present
condition, it is an anguished cry for help. "Who" is masculine;
so Paul looks for rescue from a person. "Shall deliver" is a
future tense which normally would look from the present into
the future. When this *present* is depends upon the interpreter's
view of the whole.

Nevertheless, Paul feels that his inner spirit is tied to a dead body. To me it makes the cry more poignant if it is his redeemed spirit longing to be delivered from a dead body which is still in the clutches of the sinful nature.

Verse 25 reads like the calm after a storm. Literally, "Thanks to God through Jesus Christ our Lord." Christ is the one through whom Paul gives thanks to God. God is the "who" of verse 24. The law of sin in his body still held Paul in bondage. His hope of victory in the struggle is not in keeping the law or by any effort of his own. The ascendancy of his inner self is realized only in absolute submission to God. "Jesus Christ our Lord" is not only the mediator of the apostle's thanks; he is also the one who mediates God's grace to man (see 1 Tim. 2:5).

The grace which saved us can also give us the victorious life. John 1:16 reads, "And of his fulness have all we received, and grace for grace," or "grace over against grace." It may well read "grace following grace." When Paul was saved, God did not give him a ton of grace to last throughout the remainder of his life. He continually gave him grace following after grace —an endless supply of grace. Like manna in the wilderness, a new supply of grace was his each morning—indeed, for each new trial and task. First there was saving grace; now there is sustaining grace. It is true of every Christian.

This grace gives power to live the triumphant life or to "serve in newness of spirit [Holy Spirit], and not in the oldness of the letter [of the law]" (v. 6). As long as we rely upon our own strength alone, we have only what we can do. But when, like Paul, we learn to rely upon God in Christ, we have what God can do. Many Christians live defeated lives because they never learn of the fullness of God's grace, and this grace is supplied by God the Father, on the atoning merit of the Son, and through the indwelling Holy Spirit (see 8:1–2).

Thus Paul concludes his spiritual autobiography by saying, "So now, therefore, I myself with my mind go on serving as a slave the law of God, but with my flesh sin's law" (v. 25, literal). God's law is divine law in contrast to the law of sin which dominates the flesh. The "law of God" is fulfilled in Christ. Paul realizes that while the flesh may war against his redeemed self he can win the victory only in full submission to Christ. When the Christian's desire to serve the Lord becomes greater than the desires of the flesh, he wins the victory in the conflict of desires. It is a victory not won in a day, but it is certain through him who has fully conquered the world (see John 16:33).

8

The Life in the Holy Spirit

Romans 8:1–39

Romans 8 is one of the greatest pieces Paul ever wrote. It is his most extended treatment of the Holy Spirit and his work. First Corinthians 12–14 deals more with problems in the church at Corinth which centered in the gifts of the Holy Spirit, their use and their abuse, but Romans 8 deals with the life the believer has in the Holy Spirit. Paul's emphasis upon the Spirit in this chapter is seen in the fact that the Greek word for Spirit (*pneuma*) appears only four times in Romans 1–7, but it is used twenty times in Romans 8:1–27.

The apostle has shown the struggle which rages in the believer's life between the flesh and the redeemed self. His only hope of victory over the sinful nature which still tries to control the Christian's conduct is a complete commitment of himself to God in Christ. This is made possible through the Holy Spirit who indwells him. Even while still in the flesh the believer lives in a spiritual or Spirit-filled environment as well as in a fleshly one. In fact, Paul goes so far as to say that the Christian's body is the temple, or *naos* (Holy of holies), of the Spirit of God (see 1 Cor. 6:19). So there is really no reason why he should be controlled by the sinful nature to which he has died (see Rom. 6:2).

The Freedom in the Spirit (8:1–8)

"There is therefore now no condemnation to them which are in Christ Jesus, . . . For the law of the Spirit of life in Christ Jesus hath made me free from the law of sin and death" (vv. 1–2). "Who walk not after the flesh, but after the Spirit" is not in verse 1 in the best manuscripts. However, these same words are genuine in verse 4 although the context is slightly different. Apparently some copyist borrowed from verse 4 to qualify Paul's statement in verse 1. But this freedom is in Christ through the Spirit, not dependent upon the Christian himself.

"Therefore now" (v. 1) refers to the triumphant note sounded in 7:25. In his autobiography Paul shows that he has passed from despair to joy. Although his tendency toward sin still clamors for expression in his body, he realizes that being "in Christ" or "in the sphere of Christ" there is "not even one bit of condemnation" (*katakrima*) hanging over him. He has learned to live the life that is his through "the life [*zōēs*] of the Holy Spirit" (v. 2). This he describes as another "law" that is above the law of sin and death which seeks to dominate his body. This is the "law of the Spirit of life [spiritual, redeemed life] in Christ Jesus," and it has liberated him from the law of sin and death. "Law," without the definite article in the Greek, refers to the principle or the authority by which in Christ the Holy Spirit bestows justification and life as over against sin and death. It is a great day in the life of any Christian when he realizes that he is free from the latter and lives in the former. The aorist verb form of "made free" denotes the historical moment when this took place at the point of regeneration, but the Christian must progress in his experience in Christ until he fully realizes this.

The Mosaic law was unable to effect this liberation, not because it was weak, but because human "flesh" was weak and did not live up to its demands (v. 3). "Was weak" in Greek is in the imperfect tense which means that the law was weak and continued so, but this is qualified by "through the flesh." It was a case of the spirit being willing, but the flesh being weak. The law's inability was "in which it was weak through the flesh."

For this reason God intervened through grace. "God sending his own Son in the likeness of sinful flesh, and for [concerning] sin, condemned sin in the flesh" (v. 3). "Likeness" means that Jesus had a real body of flesh (see Phil. 2:7; John 1:14), but Paul is careful not to say that there was sin in the flesh of Jesus. His flesh was real flesh, but flesh within itself is not sinful. It becomes sinful only when it is ruled by the sinful nature. Robertson (p. 372) comments about the phrase "condemned sin in the flesh" that had Paul said "the sin the one in the flesh" it would have meant that there was sin in the flesh of Jesus. But Paul was careful to avoid that idea by omitting the definite article before "in."

Christ lived in a body of flesh. He was tempted as are others, yet did not yield to temptation (see Heb. 4:15). So while his flesh was capable of sin, it was not guilty of such. In flesh Jesus proved that one can live in such a body, enduring temptation, and yet not yield to it. He proved that God is "just" in his demands upon men. Having done so, he died on the cross as the sacrifice for sin. God in Christ became the "justifier" of those who believe in his Son (see Rom. 3:26) and once and for all "condemned" (aorist tense) sin in the flesh, that is, in the flesh of Jesus. As previously shown, sin was not in his flesh, but in the death of his sinless, fleshy body God "judged down" or handed down upon sin a conviction and pronounced sentence upon it. This family of words (*katakrinō, katakrima*) is never used in the Greek papyri in a legal case ending in acquittal.

Moody (p. 214) gives a vivid picture of this. He says that flesh "is sinful only when it becomes the realm in which sin as a destructive and dangerous beast lurks and roams (7:5, 18, 25; Gal. 5:10–21). Christ from 'above' enters into the jungle of flesh 'below' to defeat sin in its own hiding place and to set free weak humanity that was sin's prey" (7:14, 23).

This was done "in order that" (*hina*) "the righteousness of the law might be fulfilled in us, who walk not after [according to] the flesh, but after [according to] the Spirit" (v. 4). Note that Paul changes from the personal pronoun referring to himself to "us," including all believers in the experience. "Righteousness" should read "ordinance" or the "requirement of the law" (RSV). Rotherham (*The Emphasized New Testament*) reads "the righteous requirement of the law." What man could not do in his own strength, God in Christ did for him. Goodspeed says that this was done in order that the law's righteous demand "might be fully met in our case." In Christ the righteous requirement of the law was met (v. 3). The indwelling Holy Spirit gives spiritual vitality whereby the Christian may have the habit of walking about (living) according to the Spirit rather than according to the flesh. Whereas in verse 1 Paul says that because we are in Christ Jesus there is no condemnation, here he reminds us that such should result in living by the Spirit rather than by the flesh. Being free from condemnation is a matter of grace, but the changed life should be evident in the way the Christian lives.

In verse 3 "flesh" refers to the material substance, but in verses 4–8 "flesh" refers to a way of life that omits God. Life according to the Spirit is a God-centered life. As previously seen, a Christian may on occasion succumb to the flesh, but in verse 4 the present tense of "walk" denotes a habitual action. The habitual action of the Christian should be according to the Spirit, not according to the flesh. Habitual life in the flesh is evidence that one is not a Christian.

Verse 5 presents the contrast between the lost person and the Christian. "For the ones being according to flesh [unredeemed] keep on putting the mind on the things of the flesh; but the ones according to the Spirit [keep on putting the mind on] the things of the Spirit" (literal). And the result? "For the mind of the flesh—death, but the mind of the Spirit—life and peace" (v. 6, literal). "Life" is eternal life which naturally results in peace.

The reason for this is that "the mind of the flesh is in a state of hostility toward God" (v. 7, literal). It is not "subject" to the law of God; neither is it able to be. "Subject" is the translation of a Greek verb denoting troops lined up and under the command of an officer. A mind at enmity toward God does not of itself have the power to submit to God. In slavery to sin it cannot serve two owners. Moody (p. 215) speaks of the mindset of the flesh as over against the mindset of the Spirit. Only as the mindset of the flesh is changed to the mindset of the Spirit can this submission to God's law be possible. It should be kept in mind that "mind" in Greek thought refers to the entire inner man; so such a change is possible only through repentance (change of heart, mind, attitude) and faith in Christ.

Paul concludes that "the ones being in flesh are not able to please God" (v. 8, literal). The ones in flesh here are the unredeemed who are enslaved to the flesh or a life devoid of God. The aorist infinitive (to please) means that they are not able to please him at any time. They are God's enemies. Their very unbelieving attitude is displeasure to him. Thus they live constantly under God's wrath. As sin's slaves they do not know the freedom that is in the Holy Spirit. Those in Christ have no condemnation; those outside him have only condemnation which is the basic reason they should know the liberation which is available in "the law of the Spirit of life in Christ Jesus."

The Indwelling Spirit (8:9–13)

Paul is continuing to discuss the theme of life in the Holy Spirit. In these verses he shows how this life is achieved, its proof, and its ultimate result. In this sense he deals with past, present, and future.

In verse 9 he assumes that his readers are not in the flesh but in the Spirit. It is one thing to live in a fleshy body. It is another thing to live under the domination of the flesh (see 7:5). One does not live in such a condition "if so be that the Spirit of God dwell in you." "Ye" is emphatic. It is written out as well as being present in the verb form. Paul has been talking of those who are "in the flesh" or are unsaved. Now in contradistinction to them he turns to those who are saved. "If so be" assumes it a fact that they are indwelt by the Spirit of God.

The indwelling of the Spirit takes place the moment one be-

lieves in Jesus as Savior (see John 14:17). His presence is
proof that one is a Christian. This is emphatically stated in
verse 9: "Now if any man have not the Spirit of Christ, he is
none of his." So the indwelling of the Spirit is, as Moody says,
"an essential, not an extra, for the Christian" (p. 216). The indwelling of the Spirit is not some future experience related to
sanctification as some interpret the word. It is instantaneous
with regeneration and simultaneously results in sanctification
or the setting apart of the believer as an instrument for God's
service. For the Christian it is a past experience. Thus Christians are called "saints," sanctified or holy ones (see 1 Cor. 1:2;
2 Cor. 1:1).

The Spirit's presence in the believer is God's seal of owner-
ship and his earnest money or guarantee of the Christian's full
redemption: regeneration, sanctification, glorification (see Eph.
1:13–14). In Acts, each time the Spirit is seen coming upon
individuals, not upon the church, it is in some way related to
their regeneration (see 8:17; 10:44; 19:6). In none of these
cases is there allowed time for a spiritual development which
would result in the *baptism* of the Holy Spirit. These comings
of the Spirit were in some way evident to the senses as proof
to the apostles that God was in this infant Christian movement.
At least in the case of the Samaritans and Cornelius, it marked
God's approval of a new development in the preaching of the
gospel. The time gap between the Samaritans' regeneration and
the coming of the Spirit upon them may be explained by the
necessity of the apostles' presence to bear witness to the fact
before the Jerusalem church. But according to John 14:17, the
normal indwelling of the Spirit is not evident to other people's
natural senses, especially those of the world, but to the inner
assurance of the regenerated person.

The present experience for the Christian is that the body
marked for death is dead through sin. It has the seed of death
in it and will, therefore, die (v. 10). But the indwelling Spirit
results in life which Denney calls "God-begotten, God-sustained
life, and therefore beyond the reach of death" (p. 646). As the
body is dead because of sin, the Christian is alive in the Spirit
because of righteousness or by being declared righteous by God.
Paul assumes this to be true as is seen in the form of condition
expressed in "if Christ be in you." This being alive because of
the indwelling Spirit infers the believer's growth in the state
of sanctification.

The future part of the Christian experience is expressed in
verse 11. The "if" clause in this verse assumes that it is true.
Since the Spirit of God, the one raising Jesus from the dead,

indwells Christians, then he who raised "Christ Jesus" (best Greek text) from the dead shall make alive their mortal bodies through his indwelling Spirit. This, of course, refers to glorification which includes the resurrection of the body (see 8:23).

"Therefore" (v. 12) refers to verses 9–11. Since the fleshly way of life produces only death (see 7:5), the Christian certainly has no obligation to live in such. "For if ye live after the flesh [in an unredeemed state], ye shall die" (v. 13), literally, "ye are about to die," or are at the point of dying. Such a way leads only to eternal spiritual death. On the other hand, "if ye through the Spirit do mortify [put to death] the deeds of the body, ye shall live" (v. 13), or have eternal life. The contrast here is between being unredeemed and redeemed. The redeemed state is evident by the indwelling Spirit.

The Sonship through the Spirit (8:14–18)

A Christian is a son or child of God. This sonship is effected by the Holy Spirit when one repents of sin and believes in Christ as Savior. Note "children of God" in verse 16. There is no difference between being sons of God and children of God.

Paul has already spoken of Christ as God's Son (see 8:3). He is God's Son essentially and eternally. People become God's sons by receiving God's Son in faith (see John 1:12). It is of interest to note that Jesus never spoke of his Sonship and his followers' sonship in the same way. He *is* God's Son. We *become* God's sons. We *become* what we once were not, but he *is* what he has always been essentially. In John 20:17 the risen Christ said, "I ascend unto my Father, and your Father; and to my God, and your God."

Moving into the matter of Christian sonship, Paul said that "as many as are led by the Spirit of God, they are the sons of God" (v. 14). Then he proceeds to show how this sonship is effected and what it involves. When Jesus spoke to Nicodemus about entering into God's kingdom and/or family, he used the vital figure of being born of the Spirit (see John 3:5). Paul says the same thing although he employs the figure of the Roman law of adoption with which his readers would be familiar.

Paul's readers did not at the moment of regeneration receive a spirit of bondage or slavery which causes one again to cringe in fear (v. 15). "But" is an adversative setting the coming idea over against the one just stated. Rather they received "the Spirit of adoption, whereby we cry, Abba, Father." "Abba" is Aramaic for "Father." *Ho patēr* (the father) translates "Abba" into

Greek (see Gal. 4:6). Most likely, all of Paul's readers could understand Greek; so the simple idea of translation hardly satisfies his usage. It could be that he used this double form as he recalled Jesus doing the same in the Garden of Gethsemane (see Mark 14:26). This would make his figure of adoption more meaningful. He is emphasizing the fact that the Holy Spirit enables the believer to call God "Father." The believer stands before God in love and peace, not as a slave stands in fear before a cruel owner.

To understand Paul's figure we must consider the Roman law of adoption. The Greek word translated "adoption" means a placing of a son, putting a person in the relation of son to a father. Under this law a person, usually a slave, could be adopted into a family as a son. This involved a ceremony, done before witnesses, and was followed by a new relationship, new privileges, and responsibilities. In the ceremony the adopting father paid a sum of money (for freedom in the case of a slave) and assumed all obligations held against the adoptee. The person then became the son of his new father, receiving the privileges and assuming the responsibilities of sonship. He became a joint heir with naturally born children. He was regarded as having been *born again* into a new family and new relationships.

All of these elements are found in Paul's figure (see Gal. 4:5–7). "The [Holy] Spirit itself [himself] beareth witness with our spirit, that we are the children of God" (Rom. 8:16). Note two witnesses. The price of redemption was paid by the Father. Thus the person in slavery to sin is freed from it. This price was not paid to the devil. It was paid by the Father to himself, as his Son's death satisfied the demands of his holy righteous nature. God assumed the freed sinner's obligations both past, present, and future. The person being adopted into God's family is born again into a new family with new relationships. He receives the privileges and responsibilities of sonship along with God's essential, eternal Son. The privileges make him an heir of God and a joint heir with Christ of all that the Father has. He also assumes the responsibilities of sonship, along with Christ—that of suffering. "If so be that we suffer with him, that we may be also glorified together" (v. 17). In the Greek text there is a play on the Greek word *sun,* meaning with: heirs *with,* sufferers *with,* glorified *with.* Note also that this covers the whole of salvation: regeneration (children); sanctification (suffering); glorification (glorified together).

Many Christians are eager to receive the privileges of sonship, but they are averse to assuming its responsibilities. Never-

theless, the two go together. Christ does not ask us to do what
he has not done. He first endured the suffering at the hands of
men. Then he received the glory which only God can give (see
Phil. 2:6–11). We often forget that this great passage in
Philippians is introduced with the words "Let this mind be in
you, which was also in Christ Jesus" (v. 5). After reading
verses 6–11 you should go back and meditate upon verse 5 or
else you will miss the purpose of Paul in the whole.

"For I reckon that the sufferings of this present time are not
worthy to be compared with the glory which shall be revealed
in us" (Rom. 8:18). Here Paul does some bookkeeping, as is
shown by the verb *reckon* (*logizomai*). This Greek word was
used for entering into a ledger (see 4:3). "Not worthy" is
emphatic in the Greek text. "Worthy" is the translation of a
Greek word (*axia*) which has in it the idea of a balance or
scales. Paul put the "sufferings of the now time," or opportune
time (*kairou*), on one side of the scales. Then he placed the
"about to be revealed glory with respect to us" (to us-ward,
toward us) on the other side of the scales. The glory so far out-
weighed the sufferings as to permit no comparison. We often
say that God balances his books. In this case Paul says that he
overbalances them in our favor. Having shared in Christ's
sufferings, we shall also share in his glory which will be revealed at his return and at the end of the age (see 1 Pet. 1:7,
13; 4:13).

The Dual Redemption in the Spirit (8:19–25)

This dual redemption is one of the strangest things that Paul
ever wrote, for it links the redemption of the created natural
order with the redemption of men. How this redemption takes
place he does not say specifically. For that matter, man's
redemption is also a mystery, but both are of God through
Christ and by the Holy Spirit.

"For the earnest expectation of the creature [created natural
order] waiteth for the manifestation of the sons of God" (v. 19).
This creation involves the entire earth and what it contains,
both animate and inanimate, other than man himself. "Earnest
expectation" is of uncertain meaning. The Greek noun is found
only here and in Philippians 1:20. The verb form is used in
nonbiblical writings. Robertson (p. 375) cites Milligan's idea
that Paul may have coined the noun. It is a compound word
formed of *apo*, off from, *kara*, head, and *dokeō*, an Ionic verb
meaning to watch. Robertson suggests the meaning is to watch
eagerly with outstretched head. Denney (p. 649) sees it as de-

noting absorbed, persistent expectation—waiting with outstretched head. J. B. Phillips renders it as "The whole creation
is on tiptoe to see the wonderful sight of the sons of God coming
into their own."

The verb translated "waiteth" means to wait eagerly and ex-
pectantly, or in suspense. It is used in 1 Corinthians 1:7 in
connection with the second coming of Christ. This same idea is
present here as seen in "the manifestation [revealing, *apoca-
lupsis*] of the sons of God." This refers to the glorification of
the saints as seen in verse 18. In a mystical way the redemption of the created natural order is related to the full redemption of men.

We must read this in the light of Genesis 3:17 where,
because of man's sin, a curse was placed upon the natural order.
"Cursed be the ground for thy sake," or because of what Adam
had done. In Eden man worked, but it was with a friendly
natural order. Now he must wrest a living from a hostile nature
(see Gen. 3:17–19). One of the features of heaven is that
"there shall be no more curse" (Rev. 22:3). We know far too
little about the relationship between the human and spiritual
and the nonhuman and natural orders to question Paul's words
at this point. We accept his teaching that as Christ's atoning
work redeemed lost man, so in a way unknown to us it also
redeems the natural order.

"For the creature [creation] was made subject to vanity, not
willingly, but by reason of him who hath subjected the same
in hope" (v. 20).

"Made subject" means to line up troops in order under a
commander. "Vanity" (empty, vain) means that the creature
did not fulfill its originally intended purpose. God created a
perfect creation for his glory. When the curse was placed upon
it, it did not fulfill this purpose. A hostile, perishing creation
cannot glorify God. True, "the heavens declare the glory of
God; and the firmament sheweth his handywork" (Ps. 19:1).
But in its overall state, creation, like man, came short of God's
glory. Now this was not done "willingly" or not of its own will.
It was not due to something nature did, but was due to man's
sin.

"Was made subject" is a passive form. The one who did this
was God. The Greek text does not attribute direct agency to
God. Rather it was God's righteous will which furnished the
occasion of it. He is not the doer of the act of making the
natural order subject to vanity, but it was "by reason of" or "on
account of" him in his righteous will. It was not a punishment
upon nature but upon man. The effect of man's sin extended

into nature. However, the effect was not without hope because this was done by the one "subjecting . . . in hope." God did not leave fallen man without hope of redemption (see Gen. 3:15), and the natural order shares in this hope.

"Because the creature [creation] itself also shall be delivered from the bondage [slavery] of corruption into the glorious liberty of the children of God" (v. 21; see v. 18). The hope mentioned in verse 20 is not God's hope but that of both man and nature. With God it is a certainty, but the fallen ones look forward to it in hope which may even be seen as "earnest expectation" (see v. 19) or assurance. With redeemed man's restored glory will come that of nature, and nature constantly holds this hope or waits upon the basis of hope. Robertson (pp. 375–76) quotes F. L. Godet to the effect that nature "possesses in the feeling of her unmerited suffering a sort of presentiment of her future deliverance."

Verses 22–23 express the deep longing in both nature and man for the full realization of this hope. "For we know [*oidamen,* absolute, perceptive knowledge] that the whole creation groaneth and travaileth in pain together until now" (v. 22). "Whole" (*pasa* without the definite article) means the whole in its several parts. Every single part of the created order suffers as awaiting childbirth, longing to give birth to the new natural order. How "we know," Paul does not say. We must remember that he wrote under divine inspiration. One cannot help but wonder if the convulsions of nature on the prowl (for example, earthquakes, floods, tornados) are a part of this. Of interest is the fact that the punishment upon Eve (see Gen. 3:16) corresponds to Paul's figure here.

But this "groaning" is also in redeemed man (v. 23). "The firstfruits of the Spirit" refer to the Holy Spirit himself. One might see this as a reference to the Spirit's coming at Pentecost. The offering of the firstfruits of ripened grain was made around the time of Passover. It looked forward to the general grain harvest about the time of Pentecost. The reference to the "body" could relate this to 1 Corinthians 15:20, where Christ's resurrection is the firstfruit pointing to the general resurrection at his return.

All of this throws light upon Paul's figure here, however, he speaks of the "firstfruits of the Spirit," not of Christ's resurrection, and, according to John 14:17 (see Eph. 1:13–14) the Holy Spirit indwelt believers prior to Pentecost. The emphasis in this chapter is upon the indwelling Spirit dating from the regeneration experience. This seems to be in Paul's mind here. Believers have experienced the "adoption" of regeneration (see

8:9, 14–17). The Spirit continues to work in them in the state of sanctification, but they groan within themselves eagerly expecting *adoption* which Paul explains as "the [full] redemption of our body" or the final bodily resurrection, which is one phase of glorification. The compound word for "redemption" should read "full redemption." It is also used in Ephesians 1:14. Thus the full redemption will then be completed in the state of glorification (see vv. 18, 30).

This redemption which began in regeneration will not be completed until the corruptible, mortal body has "put on incorruption, and . . . immortality" (1 Cor. 15:53). The soul is already saved, but at the Lord's return we shall have complete redemption—of body as well as of soul.

In verses 24–25 the apostle returns to the subject of *hope.* "For we are saved by hope" (v. 24). "The hope" (Greek) refers to a particular hope. It is the same hope as expressed concerning the natural order, but here it refers to the hope related to the Christian experience. Actually it should read, "we were saved in hope." The aorist passive form of the verb refers to a point action which from Paul's time of writing was in the past. Of course, the saving was regeneration by God in Christ through the Holy Spirit. The form of "hope" is such that it could mean "in," "by," or "for." The context seems to call for "in." We were saved in hope looking toward full redemption as seen in the resurrection of the body (see 8:11). Paul sees this as God's power acting through the Holy Spirit.

Now when one sees what he hopes for, it is no longer hope but sight. However, so long as we do not yet see it fulfilled in realization, in patient endurance we wait for it (v. 25). Thus the cycle is complete. As the believer lives in hope of the bodily resurrection, so does the natural order hope, looking toward "new heavens and a new earth, wherein dwelleth righteousness" (2 Pet. 3:13).

In this connection one should look at two other Pauline passages. In Ephesians 1:10 Paul expresses God's purpose "that in the dispensation of the fulness of times [opportune times] he might gather together in one all things [*ta panta,* the universe as a whole, both natural and spiritual] in Christ." "Gather together" is used of the segments of an army scattered in battle being reassembled under one head in order that it might become a fighting force again. Because of sin both the natural and spiritual elements of God's universe were scattered. Through God's full redemption in Christ they are again being reassembled as an orderly body under one head.

Then in 1 Corinthians 15:24–28 Paul pictures Christ reigning in his mediatorial kingdom. He is subduing ("put all things under his feet," v. 27) the universe in its several parts (*panta*, no definite article). The figure is like that in Romans 8:20 of troops being lined up in order under one head. When this has been completed with regard to the universe as a whole (*ta panta*, v. 28), Christ shall march this reassembled natural and spiritual universe into God's presence. There it and the Son will be lined up as an orderly army and will be submitted to the Father "that God [Father, Son, Spirit] may be all in all" (v. 28). This points to the time when hope shall have become sight. It will then be no longer hope but full realization—as through the Spirit God in Christ shall have accomplished his dual redemption.

The Intercession of the Spirit (8:26–27)

Not only does the Holy Spirit liberate us from the condemnation abiding in the law of sin and death by making us children of God (regeneration), and keep burning the hope of full redemption (glorification), but he also helps us in our weaknesses as we seek to cope with the matters involved in living the Christian life (sanctification). Paul illustrates this truth with the figure of prayer (vv. 27–28) and with the more general figure of all things which we encounter as God's children (vv. 28–30). The present section deals with the intercession of the Spirit.

"Likewise the Spirit also helpeth our infirmities: for we know not what we should pray for as we ought: but the Spirit itself [himself] maketh intercession for us with groanings which cannot be uttered" (v. 26). Those versed in Greek will note that the word *auto* is neuter, and the King James Version has correctly translated the word as "itself." But that misses the meaning. The word for "spirit" (*pneuma*) is neuter in gender; yet when used of the Holy Spirit it speaks of a person, so the sense in such usage is masculine gender. *Auto* agrees with *pneuma* grammatically as neuter; yet when used of the Holy Spirit it should read "himself."

Before looking at the opening clause, let us set the stage by analyzing the remainder of the verse.

Because of our weaknesses we do not really know (*oidamen*) how or for what we should pray, as it is morally and spiritually necessary (*dei*). Then the Spirit himself makes intercession for us. The verb so rendered is the usual verb "to make intercession" with the prefix *huper*, on behalf of, instead of, or as a substitute for. In such a situation the Spirit prays as our substitute or on our behalf. Robertson (p. 377) notes that this verb is found only here and in later ecclesiastical writings. It appears that Paul may have coined it. He adds that the Spirit makes intercession for us "with groanings which cannot be uttered." This is variously rendered "with unuttered groanings" or "sighs that baffle words." The idea is groanings or sighs in the spirit which are too deep to be expressed in words, or that we are unable to put into words the burden of our souls. The verb translated "intercession" in verse 27 carries the idea of coming upon one in such a condition.

Now in this situation the Holy Spirit "helpeth" our weaknesses. The short verb *helpeth* is the translation of a long Greek verb *sunantilambanomai*. It is used frequently in non-biblical Greek but occurs in the New Testament only here and in Luke 10:40. Since Luke traveled with Paul, Luke was probably familiar with Paul's use here.

Now what does this word mean? To arrive at its meaning let us break it down into its component parts. *Sun* means "with." *Anti* means "over against" (as in our prefix "anti"). *Lambanomai* means "to take." So *sunantilambanomai* means to take hold over against with someone. Suppose that you come upon someone who is trying to lift a heavy load. It is impossible for him to do it alone, so you and he get on opposite sides of the burden over against each other. Then in this position you take hold of the burden with him, and the two of you lift the load.

Applying this to prayer, the Holy Spirit does not simply pray for you, with no prayer-effort on your part. But suppose you have a burdened heart. You try to pray, but it seems that the heavens are as brass. All you seem to hear is the mocking echo of your cry. You can only groan or sigh in your soul. How many times have pastors heard people say, "I just can't seem to be able to pray any more!" In this condition the Holy Spirit comes upon you. Then he gets over against you. Together the two of you take hold and lift your burden of prayer up to the throne of grace. In so doing the Spirit puts your groanings into words. Thus your most eloquent prayer may be a groan in your soul!

Now this is possible because "he [God] that searcheth the hearts knoweth [fully knows, *oida*] what is the mind of the Spirit, because he [continually, present tense] maketh intercession for the saints according to . . . God" (v. 27). "The will of" is not in the Greek text, but this probably is the sense.

The Purpose of God's Love (8:28–30)

The remainder of Romans 8 is in the nature of a summary of God's dealings with man through the Holy Spirit. Since

"God is love" (see 1 John 4:8), all his dealings are in love. This love is evident in God's providence and purpose in history and in the lives of individual people.

"And we know that all things work together for good to them that love God, to them who are the called according to his purpose" (v. 28). This is one of the most widely loved verses of Scripture; yet, as it reads in the King James Version, it expresses not faith but fatalism. It says that somehow, someway things will turn out all right as "all things work together for good." As Moody (p. 221) says, this is more "Stoic pantheism" than "radical monotheism in which God is in charge of things!" The verb "work together" is third person singular in Greek. And while *panta* ("all things") without the definite article may read "every single part of the whole" and may be used with the singular, it does not fit Paul's emphasis upon God as the God of history (see Acts 17:24–28).

This difficulty disappears if "God" is seen as the subject of the verb "work(s) together." Two strong manuscripts (A B) use *ho theos* (God) as the subject. Both Westcott and Hort's and Erwin Nestle's Greek New Testaments use *ho theos* in brackets. However one may view the textual problem, this is the meaning as evidenced by the overall context of the Bible. God leaves nothing to chance but is guiding the stream of history toward his benevolent goal (see Rom. 8:18–27). Some would make the Holy Spirit the subject of this verb since he is seen as active in the lives of believers in this chapter (see NEB). Even if this be true, he is still God at work. Most likely "God" is the subject.

It should be noted, however, that in the Greek text the emphasis is upon the phrase "to the ones loving God"; so this is not a blanket promise to everyone. It is to those who love God. The phrase "to the ones according to his purpose being called," coming at the end of the sentence, is in the place of second emphasis. However, this is synonymous with "the one's loving God." "Know" (*oidamen*) expresses a knowledge of certainty with no reservations of doubt. So the verse reads, "For we know with a certainty that to the ones loving God, he keeps on working together with respect to every single thing unto good, to the ones according to his purpose being called."

"Working together" relates not to "every single thing" but to "the ones loving God." So as in verses 26–27 believers must be involved in the Spirit's help in praying; they must also be involved in the working. We are not simply to sit and wait passively, but as we work in the events and conditions about us, God works together with us with the ultimate goal of good.

"Purpose" (see Eph. 3:11) translates a Greek word meaning

a placing before. In both cases the reference is to God's eternal redemptive purpose. God's purpose may be seen as God's benevolent will with respect to both the natural and spiritual universe, but the emphasis here is upon redeemed people as God works in and with them through the Holy Spirit (see vv. 26–27). In the Spirit, redeemed people respond to God's love for them with their love for him. The "called" are those called out of sin into salvation.

In verses 29–30 the emphasis is upon God's loving purpose or goal for the Christian: "For whom he did foreknow, he also did predestinate to be conformed to the image of his Son, that he might be the firstborn among many brethren. Moreover whom he did predestinate, them he also called: and whom he called, them he also justified: and whom he justified, them he also glorified."

These verses grow out of "purpose" in verse 28. Indeed, they are an enlargement upon it as it pertains "to the ones loving God" or who believe in him through faith in his Son (see Rom. 4). While "purpose," or a placing before, refers to the divine council before the foundation of the world, that purpose is being worked out in the arena of history. It looks toward the consummation of the age. But since all the finite verbs in these verses are aorist tenses (point action in past time), it means that at a point in eternity these things became finished works or fully realized purpose. The evil of men and nations cannot defeat that purpose. God works together with and through his people to overrule evil as he guides history to his benevolent goal. While God is sovereign in history, this in no way violates the free will of either good or evil men. God works with the *good* and against the *evil*.

It is vitally necessary that we analyze these verses in order fully to comprehend God's purpose. The finite verbs, of course, are the key words, but other elements must be examined also. As evident in these verbs five things are involved: foreknow, predestinate, call, justify, glorify. They reach from eternity to eternity.

"Did foreknow," or "foreknew," means to know something beforehand. God is omniscient, knowing all things in himself without the need of processes of reason and knowing simultaneously all things in every point in space and time. In this sense it is logical to say that God knew beforehand who would/will be saved and who would/will be lost. This idea was first taught by Origen. Many still follow it. Indeed, it cannot be refuted. Yet it must be remembered that foreknowledge of an event does not mean that God caused it. If in your finite foreknowledge you see two automobiles on a collision course seconds before they crash, it does not mean that you either wished or caused it. The same may apply to God's infinite foreknowledge. Even though God foreknows who will or will not be saved, he does not arbitrarily cause either. While recognizing God's sovereignty, we must not ignore the equally evident fact of man's free will.

This statement was made within the context of God's love (see vv. 28, 31–39). Since "God is love" (1 John 4:8), all of God's other attributes are colored by his nature as love. So he foreknows in love. Moody (p. 221) is right in relating God's foreknowledge to his love. Eternally God loved us before we loved him (see 1 John 4:19). Foreknowledge here is related to God's children, and like an earthly father, God knows and loves his children before they know and love him. For this reason God takes the initiative in redeeming lost people. Otherwise there would be no salvation.

"Did predestinate" or "predestined" translates a verb meaning to set a boundary or a limit beforehand. The basic verb is *horizō* whence comes our word *horizon,* meaning the boundary or limit of our vision. The prefix *pro* means that God did this beforehand. Unfortunately, the English word *predestinate* has taken on a theological meaning for some, as the predetermination of every person's fate by God in his sovereignty without any recognition of man's free will. Such a position not only renders null and void the many exhortations to preach the gospel to all men, but it strikes a death blow to evangelism and missions. Furthermore, it makes God responsible for all of man's acts, including his sins—a concept which, of course, is unthinkable.

In interpreting Scripture we must consider all of it. God is sovereign, to be sure, which means that he can act in keeping with his nature without the authority, consent, or counsel of anyone outside himself. But the Bible also presents man as free to choose, even though he is responsible for his choices. Man is not a puppet on a cosmic string of fate. The Bible never presents election or predestination in conflict to man's free will.

Paul's great passage on election is found in Ephesians 1:3–14. Simply stated, before the foundation of the world God elected a plan of salvation and a people to propagate that plan. The two phases comprise most of Ephesians. God's election as to salvation is described as "in love: Having predestinated us unto the adoption of children by [through] Jesus Christ to himself" (Eph. 1:4–5). The participle "having predestinated" is the same verb as used in Romans 8:29. So God has set a boundary, like building a fence. The fence is "Christ." The phrase "in Christ" or its equivalent appears in Ephesians 1 ten times in eleven verses. So in his sovereignty God has elected to save all who are "in Christ." Each person decides in his free will whether or not to be "in Christ" (see Eph. 1:13, "believed"). Thus one may harmonize God's sovereignty and man's free will (see Herschel H. Hobbs, *New Men In Christ* [Waco: Word Books, 1974]).

In Romans 8:29 Paul shows that this boundary "in Christ" looks beyond regeneration to the development of the Christian into the likeness of Christ. "Conformed" is the translation of a compound Greek word meaning to bring to the same form or to form like. In this context it refers to an outward expression in keeping with the inward reality. A person "in Christ" grows in the state of sanctification into the "image" (*eikōn*, exact manifestation) of God's Son. This is a gradual transformation as seen in 2 Corinthians 3:18. It is an inner growth into Christ-likeness which is evident in the outward expression. This development is effected by the Holy Spirit. First John 3:2 points to the goal: "Beloved, now we are the sons of God, and it doth not yet appear what we shall be: but we know that, when he shall appear, we shall be like him; for we shall see him as he is" (see also 1 John 2:28).

The purpose of this is that Christ "might be the firstborn among many brethren." "Firstborn" does not mean that Christ is a created being. The word so translated sometimes was used as "lord" or "Lord" as in Colossians 1:15. He is the Lord of all creation. The same word is used in Colossians 1:18 where Christ is seen as "the firstborn from the dead." This is nearer to the meaning in Romans 8:29. "Firstborn" denotes prior being and preeminence. Christ is God's Son essentially and eternally. Christians have become God's sons, as Paul has shown in the figure of adoption (8:16–18). Christ is heir of God's glory. As his brothers, Christians share in his glory.

Note how Paul moves from *predestinate* to *called* to *justified* to *glorified* (v. 30). Having marked out the boundary as "in Christ," God *called* all men to be in him. Those who respond positively are *the called indeed*. These God declared *justified* before him, and these he keeps and develops, looking toward being *glorified* (the sum-total of glory and reward in heaven, including the resurrection of the body, see 8:23–25). Thus the loving redemptive purpose in eternity was/is effected in time and culminates in eternity.

The Power of God's Love (8:31–39)

With a series of questions and answers Paul reaches a climax to chapters 1–8. Having shown how God brings man from his lostness into full salvation beginning in justification and sanctification and culminating in glorification, he shows that redeemed people are kept in the power of God's love through the Holy Spirit. He still uses the form of debate with an imaginary questioner. Throughout this climax he poses questions as though raised by someone and then answers them.

"What shall we then say to these things? If God be for us, who can be against us?" (v. 31). "These things" refers to all that Paul has said beginning with 8:14. He has shown that as sons of God Christians share in Christ's sufferings and glory. The glory far outweighs the suffering. He has shown the redemptive purpose of God for both the natural creation and man, and he has shown how through the Holy Spirit God in redeeming love carries forward to completion his redemptive purpose which reaches its goal in glorification. So on this basis what shall he say? The "if" clause in verse 31 assumes that God is for (huper) us; he has acted redemptively on our behalf. Now on this basis, "who can be against us" to do us harm? Who possibly could array himself against us to our hurt? The Christian is secure, not in his own strength, but in God's.

In verse 32 "who" is the translation of two words (hos ge). Robertson (p. 148) notes that the particle ge intensifies the thought expressed. If God did not spare his own Son—his only unique Son, so very dear to him—but handed him over to be crucified "as a substitute for [huper] us all," shall he not with him give graciously [charisetai] or "freely give" us all things? God's supreme love for us is revealed in his Son. His not sparing him is a pledge to us of his infinite goodness in giving his children all things as "joint-heirs" with Christ (see v. 17).

In the second group of questions Paul establishes the fact that in Christ God's children stand blameless before him (vv. 33–34). Outside of Christ they are without excuse (see Rom. 1:20; 2:1). "In Christ" they are without blame. "Lay to the charge" translates a future indicative form of the verb meaning to impeach or to come forth as an accuser in court. The implication is that no one can do so to God's elect. "God is the one justifying" (see 3:26). Not even God will bring such a charge, and since by his judicial decree he has declared all believers in Christ as righteous, no one, not even the accuser Satan, can reverse his action.

"Who is the one condemning" (literal) or finding guilty and

pronouncing sentence? Certainly not Christ (see John 3:18). "Christ Jesus [Greek text] is the one dying, yes, rather, the one having been raised, who is on the right hand [place of first power] of God, who also is constantly interceding on our behalf" (literal; see 1 John 2:1). The Christian's assurance rests in the crucified, risen, reigning, interceding, and coming Lord. If Satan calls for our condemnation, Christ Jesus, who is our righteousness, intercedes for us. The evidence of his redeeming work is constantly before God, and as we confessed him before men, so he confesses us before the Father (see Matt. 10:32). "Confess" means to say the same thing. Before men, the believer says of Christ, "He is mine." Before the Father, Christ says of the believer, "He is mine."

This leads to the logical question: Since none can successfully accuse or condemn Christians before God, "Who shall separate us from the love of Christ?" (v. 35). This refers to Christ's love for us. Some manuscripts read "of God" (see v. 39). Denney (p. 654) on the basis of verses 28, 31, and 39 favors "of God," but he correctly adds that in any case the reference is to divine love. I see "of Christ" as the more likely reading (see v. 34). In any case, it is the love of God expressed in Christ.

Paul enlarges his question as to the "who" with a list of *whats*. "Tribulation" means to be in a tight place, like grapes in a wine press, with seemingly no way out. This list of *suffering* experiences (see 8:17–18) reads like Paul's autobiography, including even the "sword" which beheaded him, although that is still in the future for him. Since the sword was used in executing Roman citizens, this is synonymous with death and leads the apostle to cite Psalm 44:23 (v. 36). This should be the expected common lot of all Christians. It was certainly true then, and for Christ's sake Christians today should be willing to submit to it (see Matt. 16:24–26).

The Greek text does not read "nay" but "but" (*alla*, v. 37). It is used to introduce a sharply emphatic sentence. In this case it sets the question as to who shall be able to separate us from Christ's love over against verses 37–39. So this word has the effect of a denial or a negative particle.

"We are more than conquerors" is the translation of *hupernikōmen*. It is formed out of a verb meaning to conquer, with the prefix *huper,* here meaning over or beyond. It appears only here in the New Testament. Denney sees it as coined by Paul, noting his like for words with the prefix *huper.* It may be translated "superconquerors." Christians win a surpassing victory through the one who loved us (see vv. 34, 36). The suffer-

ings related in verses 35–36 serve only to bind us closer to
Christ. It is not simply suffering *for* him but *with* him (v. 17).

"I am persuaded" (v. 38) translates a perfect passive form.
It means that Paul has come to a fixed conviction. His own
experiences had played a major role in his arrival at this conclusion. Then he listed some of the things which people fear
(vv. 38–39): death, life, angels (fallen angels of whom Satan
is chief), principalities (here evil powers in the atmosphere;
"powers," *exousia,* is not in the best Greek texts), things present, things about to come, powers (*dunameis*), height (above),
depth (below), nor any other different created thing—just in
case he had not listed some fearful thing. None of these is
able or has the power to separate us from "the love of God,
which is in Christ Jesus our Lord." "To separate" translates an
aorist infinitive, to separate at any time. Blessed assurance!

After declaring the nature of the gospel at the beginning of
his letter (1:16–18), Paul really began at the bottom as he
dealt with the universal nature of sin. From the depths he
scaled the heights as he presented God's redemptive purpose
wrought in Christ and made effective through the Holy Spirit.
In 8:38–40 he reached the mountaintop. On his spiritual
Mount Everest he planted the flag of God's supremacy, a
supremacy exercised in love.

Thus he completed his presentation of the God-kind-of-
righteousness. He now turns to the matter of applying it as it
relates to certain problems. The first deals with God's purpose
as seen in his dealings with Israel and the Gentiles (chapters 9–11).

9

The Purpose of God
for Israel and the Gentiles (I)

Romans 9:1–33

As we approach chapters 9–11 we must do so with caution. Insofar as it is possible we must examine them without preconceived ideas or positions. Interpretation should be done in light of the entire Bible, with the final word spoken by God's full revelation in Jesus Christ. There must be a balance between two evident biblical truths: God's sovereignty and man's free will. Since this is a part of the Book of Romans, the interpretation must agree with the whole. It must be kept in mind that Paul is not talking about either Israel (Jews) or Gentiles as a whole. He is talking about God's purpose for both, and he deals with all men on the basis of personal faith. In fact, as my former teacher A. T. Robertson was fond of saying, we must let the Bible say what it says. *And*, in the words of W. T. Conner, professor of theology at Southwestern Baptist Theological Seminary, *it says what it means.*

In speaking of the gospel, Paul said that it was to the Jew first, and also to the Greek (see 1:16). In this order he begins his discussion of God's purpose for both.

The Concern of Paul for Israel (9:1–5)

Prior to becoming a Christian, Paul was a young shining light in Judaism. He possibly had the most promising career before him of all his immediate contemporaries in the Jewish faith. His zeal is affirmed in his record in persecuting Christians. And even though he came to be regarded as a renegade and turncoat by those of the Jewish faith, he never ceased to love them and to long for them to have a similar Christian experience to his. This evident concern is expressed nowhere more strongly than in Romans 9:1–5.

"I say the truth in Christ, I lie not, my conscience also bearing me witness in the Holy Ghost [Spirit], That I have great heaviness and continual sorrow in my heart" (vv. 1–2).

Since Paul is about to make a stupendous statement, he takes a triple oath concerning it. The first is a positive avowal: "Truth I am speaking in Christ." Note the emphatic position of "truth." The second is a negative one: "I am not lying." The emphasis is upon the negative particle, literally, "not I am lying." Third, he calls on the Holy Spirit to bear joint witness with his conscience that he is not lying but speaking truth. He took other oaths (see 2 Cor. 1:23; 11:31; Gal. 1:20), but this is his most solemn one. This is understandable in light of the gravity of what he is about to say.

He has "great heaviness" or "sorrow" (RSV) and "continual [unceasing] sorrow" or "anguish" (RSV) in his heart. His "heaviness" is the sadness of human spirit as one who mourns for the dead. "Continual" is the translation of a Greek word meaning "without leaving off." This "anguish" is consuming grief. It affects the entire body, including the heart. Robertson (p. 380) notes that it is constant pain like *angina pectoris*. All this is caused by the rejection of Christ on the part of the greater number of the Jews.

In verse 3 Paul makes the statement reflected in verses 1–2: "For I could wish that myself were accursed from Christ for my brethren, my kinsmen according to the flesh." Usually Paul uses "brethren" in the Christian sense, but here he uses it with reference to unbelieving Jews, as seen in "my kinsmen according to the flesh." "Myself" actually reads "I myself," literally, "I myself to be *anathema* from Christ as a substitute for my brethren." "Anathema" is the Greek equivalent of the Hebrew *cherem* (see Deut. 7:26; Joshua 7:12). It means something put under the ban and marked for destruction. It was used of a curse, or one accursed. Note "accursed from Christ." This does not mean simple exclusion from Christ, but cut off from him forever in eternal perdition. Denney says, "*Anathema* is to be construed with *from* Christ; the idea of separation from Christ, final and fatal separation, is conveyed" (p. 657).

Paul could have had in mind Moses' prayer in Exodus 32:32. Moses prayed for God to spare Israel, but if not, then to let him die with the sinning people. However, Paul went beyond this. He does not wish to be separated from Christ *with* but *for* (*huper*) them, as their substitute. So great is the apostle's feeling in this that he speaks of a substitutionary atonement in miniature. Of course, Christ alone could effect this. If Paul's idea seems rash, it should be recalled that it was made by one who argued so convincingly for Christ's substitutionary atonement. Furthermore, it comes from the soul-depths of one with such a great passion for his brethren by race.

Did Paul actually make this wish? The verb form translated "could wish" is the imperfect tense. Ordinarily this tense expresses a repeated action in the past or one which began in the past and continues into the present. However, the context also must be considered. Here the context is Paul's burden for Israel, on the one hand, and, on the other hand, his being *anathema* or marked for eternal perdition *away from Christ*. Furthermore, Paul speaks as a Christian who is now eternally bound to Christ in salvation (see 8:1–2). So such a separation is impossible. Also he has shown that only Christ can atone for sin and that only the Holy Spirit can effect regeneration. What the Spirit could not do—bring Israel to Christ—no sacrifice on Paul's part could do.

So the sense of the imperfect tense here seems to be that at a time in the past Paul was on the point of making such a wish, but realizing that such a result is impossible to obtain, he did not actually make it. If this were possible, he says, "I could wish that an *anathema* from Christ I myself to be as a substitute for my brethren, my kinsmen according to the flesh." W. J. Conybeare (*The Epistles of Paul*) reads, "Yes, I could wish that I myself were cast out from Christ as an accursed thing." Helen Montgomery (*The New Testament in Modern English*) says, "For I was on the point of praying to be accursed from Christ." However, knowing that all this involved an impossibility, Paul stopped short of it. Nevertheless, this does show the depth of his concern for Israel.

Verses 4–5 take up where Paul left off in Romans 3:2 in listing the advantages of the Jews over the Gentiles with regard to their relation to God. He notes that they are "Israelites" (v. 4). While "Jew" distinguishes such from "Gentile" or "Greek," "Israelites" refers to those who were members of the covenant people (Exod. 19:1–6). This implies their being a part of the theocracy (direct rule of God, or, literally, "the power of God") and partakers of the privileges inherent in the vocation as a priest-nation with its attendant promises. This was a relationship not enjoyed by Gentile nations. However, in her refusal to honor the covenant, Israel lost this peculiar position (see Matt. 21:33–45; 1 Pet. 2:1–10). This thought should be kept in mind as we proceed to examine Romans 9–11. The fact that Israel had rejected the Messiah regardless of these advantages only added to Paul's grief and anguish. He lists seven advantages of the Jews: adoption, glory, covenants, law, service, promises, and fathers.

"Adoption" carries a different meaning here than it does in 8:15. Here it refers to Israel being called God's "son" (see

Exod. 4:22–23; Deut. 32:6) and "child" (see Hos. 11:1). However, this is not in the Christian sense as in 8:14–17. "Glory" refers to the Shekinah Glory or the presence of Jehovah with his people (see Exod. 16:10; 33:18–22; 40:34; 1 Kings 8:10–11). "Covenants" (plural, some manuscripts read "covenant") —if the word be singular it could refer to Exodus 19:1–24:8 and/or Deuteronomy 29:1. The plural is probably correct. Thus one *might* see the various covenants found in the Old Testament: with Noah (Gen. 6:18; 9:9), Abraham (Gen. 12:1–3; 15:18; 17:2; Exod. 2:24), David (2 Sam. 23:5). However, the specific covenants God made with Israel are the one at Sinai (Exod. 19:1–6) and the new covenant promised in Jeremiah 31:31–34 which was inaugurated by Christ (see 1 Cor. 11:25; Heb. 8:6–9:26).

As Israel failed to keep the former covenant, she completely rejected the latter one. "The giving of the law," of course, refers to the Mosaic law. "Service" is the translation of the Greek word for priestly service as in the Tabernacle which relates to divine worship. "Promises" suggests the covenant with Abraham and its subsequent promises concerning Abraham's seed and the land of Canaan. They most certainly include the promises concerning the Messiah. The "fathers" are the patriarchs, especially Abraham, Isaac, and Jacob. It was "out of" them that Christ came "according to the flesh."

Note that Paul limits Christ's descent from the Jews to his human side, but he adds that from his divine side he is "the one being over every single part of the universe, God blessed forever," or "unto the ages" (v. 5, literal). Various views are held as to the meaning of this last phrase in verse 5. For instance, some make it simply praise to God. The RSV reads, "God who is over all be blessed for ever." Moffatt uses the parenthetical statement "(Blessed for evermore be the God who is over all! Amen.)" (See also NEB.) However, other translators refer this statement to Christ himself. Since the Greek text has no punctuation here, one will supply such as he sees it. Moody (p. 228) says, "The deity of Jesus is in no way dependent on this specific text. It is abundantly supported elsewhere" (see John 20:28).

However, Robertson renders this as in the King James Version (see also ASV and margin of RSV). Then he adds, "A clear statement of the deity of Christ following the remark about his humanity. This is the natural and the obvious way of punctuating the sentence. To make a full stop after *sarka* [flesh] (or colon) and start a new sentence for the doxology is very abrupt and awkward. See Acts 20:28 and Titus 2:13 for Paul's use of *theos* applied to Jesus Christ" (p. 381). I agree with this position. This climaxes Paul's statement about his concern for the Jews. Despite all their advantages, they rejected him who is the fulfillment of all of them—even God who came as flesh to redeem men (see 2 Cor. 5:19).

The Promise of God (9:6-13)

This promise is related to God's sovereignty and concerns the seed of Abraham which throws us back behind the Mosaic covenant upon which Israel based her claim to be God's chosen people. This was a conditional covenant of works (see Exod. 19:5-6). Israel was chosen primarily for service. The privileges as God's chosen depended upon her fulfilling the responsibility. On the other hand, the covenant with Abraham was one of grace and was, therefore, without condition (see Gen. 12:1-3). The promises concerning Canaan and Abraham's seed were related to this covenant. As previously noted, Paul sees this "seed" as Christ (see Gal. 3:16). Thus God's promise is to the true seed of Abraham—Christ—and to those believing in him.

So in verse 6 Paul anticipates the charge that "the word of God hath taken none effect" or has come to nothing. "Taken effect" is a perfect tense of a verb meaning to fall out; so the phrase means completely fallen out or failed. With an emphatic "not" (*ouch*), Paul answers this charge. Literally, "For not all the ones out of Israel [the constituted nation], these are Israel," or the true, spiritual Israel. Denney (p. 659) refers to the latter as "the people of God." Thus as Williams's translation reads, "For not everybody that is descended from Israel [Jacob] really belongs to Israel." Even the Old Testament speaks of the "remnant" of Israel (see Isa. 1:9; 10:22; 11:11, 16; 37:31; 46:3-4; Jer. 23:3; 31:7; Ezek. 6:8; 14:22; Micah 2:12; 4:7; 5:7-8; Rom. 9:27). Paul makes it clear that in the following discussion he is thinking of the true Israel which is the seed of Abraham, not by birth, but by faith (see Rom. 4; 11:26; Gal. 3:7-9).

In verse 7, to prove his point further, Paul goes back even beyond Israel to Isaac. "The seed of Abraham" included Ishmael as well as Isaac. Both were his children in the flesh. "But, in Isaac shall thy seed be called" (see Gen. 21:12-13). The "children of the flesh" are not the true "children of God" (v. 8). Only "the children of the promise are counted for the seed." This "promise" Paul identifies as that made to Abraham that "Sara shall have a son" (v. 9; see Gen. 18:10, 14; Rom. 4:17-22). God's redemptive purpose ran through Isaac. Of course, he was Abraham's son by his wife, not by a slave as was true of Ishmael by Hagar (see Gal. 4:22–31).

God's sovereign choice is most clearly seen in verses 10–13. Rebecca, Isaac's wife, gave birth to twin boys—Esau and Jacob (v. 10). According to custom the elder (Esau) would have been the one receiving the birthright and thus would be over the younger. The mainstream of the family line would have been through Esau; yet it ran through Jacob (Israel). Paul does not go into the human events which figured in the change (see Gen. 25:20–34; 27:1–41). He shows that by God's sovereign election Jacob was chosen over Esau before they were born or had done either good or evil. So the election was not based upon character but upon God's sovereign choice: "that the purpose of God according to election might stand, not of works, but of him that calleth" (v. 11). "Election" means the act of choosing or of picking out. So God said, "The elder shall serve the younger" (v. 12; see Gen. 25:23).

Finally, Paul cites Malachi 1:2–3. "Jacob have I loved, but Esau have I hated" (v. 13). This does not mean that God hated Esau emotionally. The idea of loving and hating connotes choice (see Matt. 6:24; Luke 12:46; John 12:25). Since they were twins, God had to choose one over the other through whom his redemptive purpose should run; so he chose Jacob and rejected Esau.

Now this was according to God's sovereign election or selection. It must be kept in mind that Paul is answering an imaginary Jewish questioner. This person might argue that the selection of Isaac over Ishmael, who also preceded Isaac in birth, was simple. Isaac was the legitimate heir; so Paul refers to Esau and Jacob where the opposite was true. Since the Jew claimed a special relation to God by virtue of birth and merit, Paul shows that God's selection was made before birth and apart from personal merit or deeds good or bad. This would answer the Jew's argument.

However, it must be kept in mind that the sovereign God does not ignore man's free will (see Eph. 1:4–13). Thus we cannot ignore the nature of Esau and Jacob. The picture we see of Esau is of one who lived according to the desires of his flesh. Though Jacob at the beginning was no paragon of virtue, his was such a nature that could be brought to fit into God's spiritual purpose (see Gen. 32:24–32). Like Saul of Tarsus who became Paul the apostle, Jacob became Israel, who was an instrument subservient to God's will. In his foreknowledge God knew this, and on this basis he made his sovereign choice. But man's free will was respected as seen in both brothers. Neither was a puppet but a person with the right of ultimate choice. Each was responsible for his choice. Esau made the wrong choice and lost his birthright. God did not engineer Jacob's trickery. Jacob suffered for it. But God held on to him until he was a fit person to justify and fulfill God's sovereign choice. One cannot help but see this example as the prelude to God's later dealings with Jews and Gentiles.

The Justice of God (9:14–18)

Evidently Paul's debater charged God with "unrighteousness" or injustice in his sovereign dealing with Esau and Jacob (v. 14). Paul's reply is seen in the second question, the form of which calls for a negative response. He repudiates the idea with his familiar "God forbid!" To fortify it he cites a case from Moses' life (v. 15).

Israel had sinned in worshiping the golden calf (see Exod. 32). Moses prayed that God would not destroy the people. In a dialogue with God Moses asked to see God's face as evidence that he would lead Israel into Canaan. Unable to see God's face, Moses was promised a view of God's glory. It would be granted, not on the basis of Moses' merit, but on the basis of God's goodness and grace. Thus God said, "I will have mercy on whom I will have mercy, and I will have compassion on whom I will have compassion" (v. 15; see Exod. 33:19).

The question was raised concerning God's justice. Paul answers by showing God's mercy and compassion. Had a sovereign God shown justice alone, Israel would have perished. Instead, he demonstrated his mercy and compassion in forgiveness. So sovereignty can work either way. Verse 16 shows that the sovereign act of God was one of grace. It is not dependent upon the one wishing or striving but upon a merciful God. Note, however, that God also respected man's free will: the people returned to the worship of Jehovah after Moses' prayer for them (see Exod. 32:32; 33:10).

From the bright side of God's sovereign election, Paul turns to the dark side. For this he uses the example of Pharaoh (v. 17; see Exod. 9:16). The purpose of Pharaoh's existence was that God might demonstrate his power in delivering Israel from bondage and that God's name might be declared throughout the earth. This is true even today as we see divine intervention on behalf of his people. Pharaoh as God's adversary is a balance for Moses as God's servant. As Moses and Israel could receive mercy, Pharaoh could not. Denney says that Pharaoh "was the open adversary of God, an avowed, implacable adversary; yet a Divine purpose was fulfilled in his life, and that purpose and nothing else is the explanation of his very being" (p. 662).

"Therefore hath he mercy on whom he will have mercy, and whom he will he hardeneth" (v. 18). "Will" in both cases translates the Greek verb meaning to will or wish. This verse refers to both Moses and Pharaoh. The verb translated "hardeneth" means to make hard, to render obstinate or stubborn.

This case of Pharaoh causes some difficulty. Did God arbitrarily harden his heart? Certain passages in Exodus attribute Pharaoh's hardness to God (see 4:21; 7:3; 9:12; 10:1, 20, 27; 11:10; 14:17), but others say that Pharaoh hardened his own heart (see 7:14, 22; 8:15, 32; 9:34). For his purpose Paul chose the former incidents, but from the above references we see man's free will as well as God's sovereignty involved. God did not arbitrarily give to Pharaoh his obstinate, rebellious will. He does not perpetrate man's sin (see James 1:13). The Egyptian ruler's sinful nature did this (see James 1:14). Wuest expresses it correctly: "When God is said to harden Pharaoh's heart, it is that He by demanding the release of Israel, confronted him with an issue which he did not wish to meet" (p. 163). Moody notes that as the law revealed sin already present, "God's word to Pharaoh brought out a hardness of heart already present" (p. 231). The same gospel of Christ produces different results in different people (see 2 Cor. 2:16).

So by the examples of Moses and Pharaoh, Paul demonstrates that in his sovereignty God shows both mercy and justice— mercy where man's free will makes it possible; justice where man's free will makes it necessary. In both cases God acts in a manner true to his nature and without the counsel or consent of anyone outside himself.

The Free Hand of God (9:19–26)

This is actually a continuation of the thoughts expressed in verses 14–18. Paul imposes an imagined interruption by his questioner which is based upon the figure of Pharaoh. It still raises the question as to God's justice.

The questioner's objection to Paul's argument sets man's free will over against God's sovereignty. If God is sovereign, what happens to human freedom? This is expressed in two questions. "Why doth he yet find fault? For who hath resisted his will?" (v. 19). If God hardened Pharaoh's heart, why does he blame him for his actions? Who can successfully stand against God? These questions may also refer to the present time.

"Hath resisted" is the translation of the perfect tense (indicating completeness) of the Greek verb meaning "to stand" with the prefix "against" (*anti*). Many have tried to resist God's will, but the idea in this word is more the result than the process. One may resist God's will, but he cannot maintain it successfully. Such effort ends only in tragedy for the one resisting. However, if God is sovereign, how can he in justice lay blame upon the sinner? This is a legitimate and unanswerable question if we ignore man's free will. In such a case God, not man, is to be blamed for human sin. This itself is unthinkable!

Paul answers his critic with a longer series of four questions (vv. 20–24). First, "Nay but, O man, who art thou that repliest against God?" (v. 20). In the Greek text there is no negative "nay," but the idea is present in a complex use of particles: *men*, indeed, *oun*, therefore, *ge*, at least. Robertson translates it "O man, but surely thou who art thou?" "Man" is contrasted with "God." "Repliest" renders a participle of a compound verb meaning to give off a judgment against, to answer in contradiction or contention. Mere man daring to do this to God.

The second question is, "Shall the thing formed say to him that formed it, Why hast thou made me thus?" (v. 20). The form of this question invites a negative answer. "The thing formed" (*to plasma*, from which we derive the English words *plasma* and *plastic*) means something molded out of mud or wax. It is unheard of that the thing formed should so question the one forming it (see Isa. 29:16).

Third, "Hath not the potter power over the clay; of the same lump to make one vessel unto honour, and another unto dishonour?" (v. 21). This question is anticipated in verse 20. It is a familiar figure in the Old Testament—God as the potter and man as the clay (see Isa. 45:9; 64:8; Jer. 18:1–6). Wuest (pp. 165–66) quotes Vincent as to the biblical (Gen. 2:7) and primitive accounts elsewhere throughout the earth as to the formation of man out of dust or molded earth. From the same lump of clay a potter may make one vessel of honor (a dish for food) and another of dishonor (a garbage recepticle). The objection that "a man is not a pot" (C. H. Dodd, *Romans*) hardly holds here. Paul's figure is drawn from Scripture and is apt for his purpose to liken man's objection to God's sovereign purpose. Infinitely more than the potter, God is free to use his hands to mold men as he wills in order to fulfill his purpose. However, it should be noted that in the final question where Paul applies his figure to men, the free will of man is evident.

Fourth, "What if God, willing to shew his wrath, and to make his power known, endured with much longsuffering the vessels of wrath fitted to destruction: And that he might make known the riches of his glory on the vessels of mercy, which he had afore prepared unto glory, Even us, whom he hath called, not of the Jews only, but also of the Gentiles?" (vv. 22–24).

In these verses the apostle moves from the figure to its application, from inanimate objects to people. The principle of God's sovereignty or free hand still applies, but here Paul shows that, in keeping with God's nature, it is tempered by his mercy and longsuffering. As a holy, righteous God he wills to show his wrath and power against sin, but he withholds such in "much longsuffering." Note that Paul uses *orgē* for wrath, God's abiding, universal opposition toward evil (see 1:18). *Thumos*, a sudden outbreak of anger which soon subsides, would not fit with "much longsuffering." God's *orgē* is nonetheless real. In fact, it is all the more terrible when his longsuffering comes to an end. But though his wrath and power against sin are real, God waits. This is an evidence of his mercy as he gives opportunity for repentance (see 2:4–11).

The key word in verse 22 is the one translated "fitted" (*katērtismena*), a perfect participle. It is used of "vessels of wrath fitted [made, RSV] unto destruction." Does this mean that they were so destined from the beginning? If so, why does God wait before showing his wrath and power? Worthy of note is the fact that the verb translated "had afore prepared" in verse 23 has the prefix *pro*, "before." It is absent from the verb "fitted" in verse 22.

The perfect tense expresses the idea that these vessels or people were fitted for destruction at some past time, a condition which still stands. Moody comments: "A certain stage on the way toward destruction has been reached" (p. 231). He also notes that this participle may be either passive or middle (reflexive) voice. If the former be read, it means that God did it to men. If the latter be seen, it means that they did it to themselves. Had Paul meant the former he could have used another verb "prepared beforehand" (*prokatartizō*). Reading this as a middle voice means that God showed much longsuffering toward those who through sin and hardened hearts had made themselves vessels of wrath prepared for destruction. This coincides with God in his sovereignty respecting man's free will, and it agrees with Romans 2:4–11. God's wrath and power will. be shown all the greater when, after being stored up, it finally breaks upon them.

The Twentieth Century New Testament reads "the objects of his displeasure, though they were fit only to be destroyed." The Berkeley Version reads "the agents that deserve wrath and are maturing for destruction." Moffatt seems to have caught Paul's meaning. "What if God, though desirous to display his anger and show his might, has tolerated most patiently the objects of his anger, ripe and ready to be destroyed?" (9:22). This overall analysis agrees with God's sovereign wrath and power against sin, his longsuffering and mercy which desires man's repentance and salvation, man's free will, and the certainty of destruction (not annihilation) of the persistently unrepentant. This blends with the overall teachings of the Bible.

The thought in verse 23 is not so difficult to interpret. However, it should be noted that "had afore prepared" does not mean that man's free will is ignored. Salvation and glory are God's will in election and predestination, but they are for those who through faith in Christ respond positively to God's gracious offer. This is in agreement with the larger context of Romans, indeed, of the New Testament.

All which precedes verse 24 (9:6–23) points to "even us, whom he hath called, not of the Jews only, but also of the Gentiles." So Paul at this juncture enters into the heart of the problem of Jews and Gentiles. The *called*, of course, are those who have in faith responded to God's call. The call was issued to all men regardless of race or other human distinctions. This call was issued through the gospel (see 10:14–18). Paul's concern is not that so many Gentiles, but that so few Jews responded favorably to the call.

In support of his contention that Gentiles, as well as Jews, are included in God's saving purpose, Paul cites the Book of Hosea (vv. 25–26; see Hos. 1:6–10; 2:23). "Not my people" refers to *Lo-ammi*, the Hebrew for "not my people" (Hos. 1:9). "Not beloved" refers to *Lo-ruhamah* (Hos. 1:6) meaning "no mercy" or love. These references reflect Hosea's mercy and love in accepting as his own two illegitimate children born to his faithless wife. Eventually she left him, finally became a prostitute, and then was so worthless as to be sold as a slave. At God's command Hosea bought (redeemed) her and took her to his bosom. This lesson to Hosea about Israel Paul applies to the Gentiles. Gentiles were not God's *chosen* (not my people). Jews regarded them as outside God's love and mercy (not beloved), but God's redemptive purpose includes both believing Gentiles and Jews. All such shall be called "the children of the living God."

The Remnant of God (9:27–29)

Paul has already alluded to God's faithful remnant in the nation of Israel (see 9:6). Now he specifically speaks of them

in two quotations from Isaiah (vv. 27–28—Isa. 10:22–23; v. 29
—Isa. 1:9; see Hos. 1:10).

In the former passage, Isaiah prophesies that a few people
of Judah would escape the disaster of Jerusalem at the hand
of Sennacherib. Paul applies this prophecy to the believing Jews
who will be saved. The name of Isaiah's son, Shearjashub,
means "a remnant shall return" (see Isa. 10:21). Verse 28 is
used to declare the certainty of God's work concerning the remnant, or the Jews who receive Christ as Savior.

The latter passage from Isaiah assures Paul's readers that
the "seed" or remnant ("the mere germ of a nation," NEB) will
remain, and out of it shall go the gospel to all men in order that
God's redemptive purpose shall be accomplished. Ronald Knox
translates this, "If the Lord of Hosts [Sabaoth] had not left us
a seed to breed from." This seed, of course, is the spiritual seed
of Abraham through faith (see 9:7). Not all Jews will be saved;
not all Gentiles will be saved. But out of saved Jews and Gentiles God is fulfilling his promise made to Abraham that the
world will be blessed through his "seed" (Christ) and all who
believe in him. These form the true, the spiritual Israel—Christians—"which in time past were not a people [constituted na-
tion], but are now the people of God" (1 Pet. 2:10). These are
those who are redeemed to God by Christ through his blood
"out of every kindred, and tongue, and people, and nation"
(Rev. 5:9).

The Centrality of Christ (9:30–33)

The redemptive purpose of God centers in Christ. God the
Father proposed redemption. God the Son provided it. God the
Holy Spirit propagates it. Of course, in each phase of the redemptive process it is God in his triune revelation who works
all things for the accomplishment of his purpose. Nevertheless,
whether or not we are rightly or wrongly related to God rests
in our response to Christ because by God's sovereign will the
God-kind-of-righteousness is bestowed upon those who believe
in his Son. So before dealing with the Gentiles and Jews as such,
Paul shows the centrality of Christ in the matter.

"What shall we say then? That the Gentiles, which followed
not after righteousness, have attained to righteousness, even the
righteousness which is of faith. But Israel, which followed after
the law of righteousness, hath not attained to the law of righteousness" (vv. 30–31).

The church in Rome was largely Gentile in nature. The Jewish Christians might well ask why this was true since Israel was

a chosen or elected people. This same question could be raised about all the churches throughout the predominantly Gentile world. So following his adopted style in Romans of a debate with an imaginary Jewish questioner, the apostle deals with this question.

"Followed after" in both verses may read "pursued" (RSV). Moffatt uses the words "aimed at," but pursued or chased after is better. The Gentiles did not pursue righteousness, but they attained it. The Greek verb translated "have attained" means to grasp or seize so as to make something one's own. Agreeing with *pursued* it connotes the idea of overtaking righteousness, a righteousness growing out of "the faith," or faith in Jesus Christ.

On the other hand, Israel also pursued righteousness, specifically, "a law kind of righteousness." "But" is adversative, setting Israel over against Gentiles. However, rather than laying hold of it to make it their own, the Jews did not *arrive* at it. They thought of righteousness in terms of law, not of grace through faith. In the Mosaic law they had such a law, but no matter how rapidly they pursued it, its standard eluded their grasp. When they had done their best, humanly speaking, there was more beyond in the demands of law. So they did not arrive at its goal. It remained beyond their reach. To achieve righteousness by law demanded perfect obedience, which, of course, they did not give. A religion of legalism proved to be a failure. Both uses of "law" in verse 31 are without the definite article in the Greek. While here Paul has the Mosaic law in mind, the sense may apply to any form of legalism.

The God-kind-of-righteousness is not to be chased by legalism but received by faith. It is not man-centered but God-centered; it is a gift received from and not a debt paid by God. Legalism leads to death; faith results in life.

"Wherefore? Because they sought it not by faith, but as it were by the works of the law" (v. 32). "Of the law" is not in the best manuscripts. Literally, "Because not out of faith [as the source], but as if out of works" as the source (see Eph. 2:8–10).

In verses 32–33 (literal) Paul explains why the Jews did not lay hold upon the God-kind-of-righteousness. "They stumbled at the stone of stumbling; as it is written and stands written [perfect tense], Behold, I lay in Sion a stone of stumbling and a rock of offence [*skandalon*, see 1 Cor. 1:23, scandal]: and the one believing on him not shall be ashamed" (see Isa. 8:14; 28:16; Matt. 21:42; 1 Pet. 2:6–8). Isaiah 28:16 reads "shall not make haste." Paul for his own purpose says "shall not be ashamed." Those believing in Christ shall not be disappointed or put to shame in not laying hold upon the God-kind-of-righteousness.

In Paul's day it was considered legitimate to mix Scripture quotations so long as it did not violate the truth expressed. A good example of this is found here. Isaiah 8:14 reads "rock" (Greek, *petra,* see Matt. 16:18) and "a stone of stumbling" (Greek, *proskomma*). Paul uses these in his quotation of Isaiah 28:16. A *proskomma* was a smaller stone like a boulder which could be rolled across a path. A *petra* is a large ledge rock or outcropping of bedrock, the top of which might stick up through the ground. But in either case it could cause a person to stumble.

Some interpreters see this stumbling stone as faith in Christ, and others see it as Christ himself. If I must choose, I would select the latter, but there seems to be little difference in the ultimate meaning, for faith here is faith in a person—Christ.

With their preconceived ideas about their relation to God and about the nature of the Messiah as a political-military figure, the Jews stumbled over a crucified Christ (see 1 Cor. 1:23). Furthermore, they saw in the demand for faith in him a repudiation of their entire religious experience and system. To them it meant beginning all over again, starting from the foot of a cross and from the door to an empty tomb, the meaning of the latter of which was denied by their religious leaders (see Matt. 28:11–15). They did not see that Jesus Christ was their Messiah for whom they prayed and waited. They did not realize that he was no iconoclast but the fulfillment of all that was true in Judaism—the one filling full the meaning of their Scriptures. So they as a group largely rejected the Christ of God, an unspeakable tragedy. It is no wonder that it gave Paul heaviness of spirit and anguish of heart. It should do the same to each Christian, stirring up within him the desire that every Jew and every Gentile would receive Christ and be saved.

10

The Purpose of God
for Israel and the Gentiles (II)

Romans 10:1–11:36

The heart of Paul's treatment of God's purpose for Israel and the Gentiles is found in Romans 10–11. The principles discussed in chapter 9 are applied in the remainder of this discussion.

The Failure of Israel (10:1–21)

Despite the advantages which the Jews enjoyed over the Gentiles in their relation to God (see 3:1–2; 9:4–5), they failed to attain the God-kind-of-righteousness. They stumbled over Christ (see 9:31–33) and failed in their own efforts to obtain the righteousness which God demands.

In Romans 10:1 Paul repeats his concern for the Jews. The desire of his heart and his supplication to God was "unto salvation," or with respect to salvation for Israel. Though the Jews had rejected Christ, Paul does not feel that their case is hopeless. Had he considered the Jews entirely reprobate, he would not have prayed for them, but he prays for them for three reasons.

First, "they have a zeal for God" (v. 2, RSV). God is the object of their zeal. "Zeal" comes from a Greek word meaning to burn. The Jews were on fire for God. Paul bears witness to this fact. "I bear record" (*martureō*) was used of giving testimony in court. From his own personal experience Paul testifies to the zeal of Jews toward God (see Acts 22:3; Gal. 1:13–14), but he adds that it is not "according to [full] knowledge." The Greek word translated "knowledge" is a compound word for experiential knowledge. They knew about God, but they did not fully know him with respect to his righteous demands and redemptive purpose in Christ.

Zeal without full knowledge produces fanatics—then and now. It must be guided by understanding if it is to accomplish the proper result. Like Saul of Tarsus these fanatical Jews thought they were serving God in opposing Christ and the gospel. There is no fanaticism so great and destructive as that which is rooted in a false or partial knowledge of religion.

Second, the Jews were without knowledge of the God-kind-of-righteousness (v. 3). In Greek the word for "without knowledge" is emphatic. They were seeking to establish their own by their good works. Theirs was a seeking through legalism, not a receiving by faith. The result was that "to the righteousness of God they did not submit," or line up as troops under a commander. Note the emphatic position of "the righteousness of God" in contrast to "their own righteousness." It is the difference between a God-centered and a man-centered righteousness. With their emphasis in the wrong direction, their very zeal carried them away from God.

Third, the focal point of Paul's prayer is Christ in his relation to law. He is "the end of the law for [unto] righteousness to every one that believeth" (v. 4). The emphatic word is "end" (*telos*). It may mean fulfillment or goal. Christ came not to abolish the law but to fulfill it or fill it full of meaning (see Matt. 5:17). The laws of sacrifice are fulfilled in his once-for-all-sacrifice (see Heb. 10:1–14). He taught the spirit, not merely the letter, of the moral law (see Matt. 5:17–48), and as *goal,* the entire Old Testament pointed to him.

But he is the "end" of the law only to those who believe in him. God's righteousness was established in him. It is available to all who receive him as Savior. So the emphasis here is upon the fact that Christ inaugurated a new way of salvation. Not simply those who do the works of law are declared righteous by God, but those who receive his righteousness in Christ (see 3:20–26).

Beginning in verse 5 Paul contrasts legal righteousness with the righteousness of God in Christ. Moses said of legal righteousness "that the man which doeth those things shall live by them" (v. 5; Lev. 18:5). But, as previously seen, such must do them perfectly. That is why God offers his righteousness in Christ.

"But" (v. 6) sets the following over against verse 5, literally, "But the out-of-faith righteousness says thus, 'Say not in thine heart, Who shall ascend into heaven?'" to bring Christ down from heaven to earth. In the Incarnation he has already come to earth as Jesus of Nazareth. But the Jews as a whole rejected him. Neither should one say, "Who shall descend into the deep?" to bring Christ up from the dead (v. 7). He has already risen from the dead. "Deep" is the translation of a Greek word meaning "abyss" or a bottomless hole. In Revelation 9:1 it is used of the place of torment. However, to say that at his death Christ entered into hell as a place of torment is to misread Scripture. In Acts 2:27 Peter quotes Psalm 16:10. The Hebrew reads *sheol,* and the Greek reads *hades.* These referred to the abode of the dead, not to a place of punishment as such. In 1 Corinthians 15:55 "grave" is the translation of *hades.*

Two thoughts stand out in these verses. The incarnation and resurrection are not man's work but God's work. Also the Jews are not to look to the future but to the past for God's mighty work of redemption. It has already taken place and only waits for their personal faith for it to be effected in them. Sadly, as a people the Jews reject this work of God. They speak of Jesus as a prophet but nothing more. The Mohammedans do the same. The Jews still look for their Messiah when he has already come!

"But what saith it?" (v. 8). "It" refers to verse 6. Compare Romans 10:6–7 with Deuteronomy 30:11–14, and you will see that Paul borrows language from Moses to speak Christian truth. This was a legitimate literary device then. In this light we can understand Paul's words in verse 8. The *saying* of the righteousness of faith is near them, on their lips, and in their hearts or minds. It is "the word of the faith, the one we are proclaiming." As a former Pharisee Paul speaks to Pharisees whose emphasis is upon legalism rather than upon "faith." "The faith," of course, refers to a particular faith, the Christian faith or that which centers in Christ. Paul did not deal in philosophical speculation but in a Person and in an actual historical event. The event was the death and resurrection of Christ by which God set in operation in history his eternal redemptive purpose. To be saved one must believe in the Person and in the event involved, but ultimately it must be faith in a Person. This Person-event is declared in verses 9–10: "That if thou shalt confess with thy mouth the Lord Jesus, and shalt believe in thine heart that God hath raised him from the dead, thou shalt be saved. For with the heart man believeth unto righteousness; and with the mouth confession is made unto salvation."

Note that Paul places the *Person* before the *event.* And as Moody (p. 236) notes, the Hebrew parallelism used by Paul in both verses "makes confession and belief, as well as righteousness and salvation, two sides of the same coin (Matt. 12:34–37; Luke 6:45)." One does not truly confess what he does not believe. If he really believes, he will confess. The New Testament does not teach secret discipleship.

"Lord Jesus" is not just so many words to be repeated glibly. Since the Greek has no definite article, it may read "Jesus as Lord" or "Jesus is Lord." Those who worshiped Roman emperors said, "Lord Caesar," or *Kurios Kaisaros*. Refusing to say this, Christians said, *Kurios Iēsous*. Christians were persecuted, some even unto death, because of this. To confess "Lord Jesus" involved more than simply uttering words. It came to be a matter of life and death.

However, at the time Paul wrote Romans, his use of this term should be seen more in its Jewish than in its Roman setting.

"Jesus" (*Iēsous*) is the Greek equivalent of the Hebrew "Joshua" (*Yeshua*) which means "Jehovah is salvation" or "Jehovah saves." "Lord" (*Kurios*) was used in the Greek translation of the Old Testament (Septuagint) to translate the word for "Jehovah" (*Yahweh*), the peculiar name for the true God of Israel. It is his saving name (see Exod. 3:7–22, especially v. 14; literally, "He will be that [which] he will be"; Jehovah was revealing himself as the one redeeming Israel from bondage). When used of Jesus in the strictly Christian sense, it means that he is Jehovah in flesh for man's salvation. No Jew would confess "Lord Jesus" who did not really believe it. No Gentile would do so who still called Caesar *Lord*. Paul says that no one calls Jesus Lord except by the Holy Spirit (see 1 Cor. 12:3).

In verse 9 "confess" is mentioned before "believe." In verse 10 the order is reversed. This latter is the logical order. "Confess" is the translation of a Greek word which means to speak the same thing. So to confess Jesus as Lord means that one believes the biblical record about Jesus and all that it involves. It is specifically a confession of faith in the full deity of Jesus and a commitment to him as Lord. Many people are willing to confess Jesus as Savior but are reluctant to receive him as Lord. The two belong together. It is "Lord Jesus" or "Jesus as Lord." Verse 11 is a repetition of a portion of Paul's quotation of Isaiah 28:16 in 9:33.

This promise of verses 9–11 is for both Jews and Greeks (Gentiles). God is no respecter of persons. He is rich in forgiving grace to all who call upon him (v. 12). "For whosoever shall call upon the name of the Lord shall be saved" (v. 13; see Joel 2:32). God's only way of salvation is through the Lord Jesus. Moody (p. 237) says, "Joel meant the Lord of the covenant when he said Lord, and Paul meant no less when he applied the name to Jesus (Phil. 2:6–11)." Worthy of note is the lavish use of the Old Testament which Paul makes in these words about the failure of the Jews. It should also be noted, however, that verses 12–15 refer to Gentiles as well as Jews.

Verses 13–15 form a strong appeal for missions to all men. The repeated reference to "they" draws upon the "whosoever" (*pas*, every single one). To be saved, each one must call upon the name of the Lord. "Name" stands for the person. In this series of questions Paul repeats the second verb of each question in the next one. People do not call upon someone for salvation without having believed in him. They will not believe in someone of whom they have not heard. They cannot hear without a preacher. For one to preach he must be *sent forth*. "Send forth" is the translation of the Greek verb from which comes the word for "apostle." This suggests that at this point Paul was thinking of his own apostleship to the Gentiles. The words "preacher" and "preach" translate a Greek root meaning to act as a herald. It was used with reference to one who announced the participants in and the results of athletic events (see 1 Cor. 9:27). More to the point here is to act as a king's herald. God's people were to hear and heed as if the king spoke in person (see 2 Cor. 5:20). Paul closes this missionary appeal by quoting Isaiah 52:7 (v. 15).

The question is raised as to whether Paul was thinking of evangelism among Jews or Gentiles. In light of verse 12 he evidently had both in mind, even though he resumes his thoughts about Jews in verse 16. In fact verses 16–21 also include both Jews and Gentiles. Paul is anticipating his treatment of Jews and Gentiles in chapter 11.

"But they have not all obeyed the gospel" (v. 16). The words "glad tidings" and "gospel" both translate Greek words from which comes the English word *evangelism* or good news. To give scriptural support to this statement the apostle quotes Isaiah 53:1. The fact is that Israel has heard but has not believed. She had the proclamation but refused it. Certainly she heard the gospel in the Suffering Servant passages of Isaiah climaxed by Isaiah 53, to·say nothing of the gospel in the Christian era. But to both she turned a deaf ear. Thus she is responsible before God for her rejection of Christ. So Paul concludes that "the faith comes out of hearing, and the hearing through the word of Christ," or "the word about Christ" (literal). ("Christ," not "God," is in the best manuscripts.) "The faith" refers to a particular faith, faith in Christ, and it comes out of that which is heard. The proclamation of the gospel engenders faith through the Holy Spirit's power, but even he will not violate man's free will by forcing faith upon him.

Emphasizing the fact that Israel has heard, Paul says, "Their sound went into all the earth, and their words unto the ends of the world" (v. 18; see Ps. 19:4). Although the psalmist was writing of God's revelation in nature, Paul can apply it to the gospel (see Col. 1:6, 23). "World" translates a Greek word meaning the inhabited earth, but, as here, it was used to refer

to the Roman Empire. Robertson (p. 390) notes that the very
sound of the word for "sound" (*phthoggos*) is that of the vibra-
tion of a musical string. Being sounded first in Jerusalem, the
gospel vibrations have been heard throughout the Roman Empire, and so wherever Jews dwell in that empire (the *Diaspora*,
dispersion of Jews).

Paul asks a second question. "Did not Israel know?" (v. 19).
"Know" here means to know by the experience of hearing.
Robertson translates the two questions in verses 18–19, "Did
they fail to hear?" and "Did Israel fail to know?" In each case
a negative answer is expected. To put it positively, Israel did
hear and know, but she failed to believe. In three quotations
from the Old Testament Paul shows that Israel knew even before Christ came (v. 19, Deut. 32:21; v. 20, Isa. 65:1; v. 21,
Isa. 65:2). Both Moses and Isaiah told the Jews that because of
their rebellion against him, God would turn to the Gentiles
(vv. 19–20). And Isaiah adds that despite God's constant call,
Israel remained "a disobedient and gainsaying [talking back]
people" (v. 21). They were both contrary and contradictory,
and this continued in their reaction to God's revelation in his
Son. Thus Paul shows conclusively the failure of Israel to avail
herself of the opportunity despite her privileged position with
God.

The Saved Remnant (11:1–10)

In chapter 9 Paul showed that God is sovereign. In chapter 10
he has declared that Israel has sinned but that Gentiles received the gospel, which shows that a sovereign God respects
man's free will. Now in chapter 11 he combines the two ideas
of Jews and Gentiles to show that in God's sovereign will he
proposes to save both—based, of course, upon their faith in
Christ. This chapter reflects 8:28, that God works in all circum-
stances for good to those who love him and respond to his call
to salvation.

Continuing his style of debate with an imaginary questioner,
Paul strongly repudiates the idea that because of Israel's repeated refusals God has "cast away" his people (v. 1). The
question invites a negative answer. This is strengthened by
"God forbid!" "Cast off" translates a Greek verb in the middle
(reflexive) voice. It means to push away from oneself, to repel
or repudiate. The truth is that Israel repudiated God, but, even
so, God has not given up on them. As "an Israelite, of the seed
of Abraham, of the tribe of Benjamin," Paul himself is proof
that Israel has not been cast away. If that had happened, even

Paul, to say nothing about thousands of other Christian Jews, would have been cast off.

But who are "his people"? Wuest quotes De Wette to the effect that Paul has national Israel in mind (pp. 185–86). However, this is contrary to Romans 9:6. The tone of Paul's discussion throughout Romans is that the true seed of Abraham are those of faith in God's promise. Of course, De Wette sees a future national turning of Jews to Christ. One hopes so, but this is speculation (see Acts 15:11). Not all Jews will be saved, just as not all Gentiles will be saved. God is no respecter of persons (see Acts 10:34; Rom. 2:11; Eph. 6:9; Col. 3:25). First Peter 2:1–10 clearly shows that those who are "now the people of God" are those out of every nation who have received Christ as Savior. That those are "his people" who have exercised faith toward God is evident from Paul's discussion of the remnant idea.

"God hath not cast away his people which he foreknew" (v. 2; see 8:29–30). Then Paul proceeds to show from the Old Testament that "his people" among Israel are the remnant of faith. He could have cited such passages as Isaiah 1:9, 9:12, 10:22, Jeremiah 23:3, Amos 9:8–10, Micah 2:12, 5:3, and Zephaniah 3:12–13. Of course, the primary reference is to the return of the remnant to Palestine after the exile, but these verses do serve to show that they are not all Israel which are of Israel (Rom. 9:6).

First, Paul chooses the case of Elijah, one of the earlier prophets (1 Kings 19:10, 14, 18). Elijah felt that he alone was true to Jehovah, but God reminded him of seven thousand in Israel who had not worshiped Baal. They were the remnant because they remained faithful to Jehovah. So as the *Oxford Annotated Bible* says, "Paul as a Jew is no more alone than Elijah was." Though the mass of Jews rejected Christ, a remnant of thousands of Jews have believed in him as Savior, and these are a part of the true Israel.

"Even so then at this present time also there is a remnant according to the election of grace" (v. 5). "Remnant" means that which is left. Though the mass of Jews repudiated God in Christ, these were left who received God's redemption in Christ. "Election" or a choosing out is qualified by "grace." God elected to save by grace those who received his Son. This remnant had done so. "Is" translates the perfect tense of the Greek verb "to become." By faith in Christ and by God's grace, they became and still are the remnant of Jews who are a part of the host of the saved. Verse 6 simply says that grace and works cancel out each other. You cannot be saved by works and grace. Grace is

God's gift. If any part of salvation is by works or personal merit, then grace ceases to operate. And since God's sovereign will is to save by grace, works do not in any sense avail. The failure of the mass of Jews was at this point (see 10:2–4), but the remnant has been saved by grace through faith, even as have Gentiles. The best Greek texts do not have the latter half of verse 6, but it does not change the sense.

"What then?" (v. 7). If God has not cast away his people, what happened to them? Israel as a whole "keeps on seeking" righteousness but has not obtained it (see 10:2–3). However, the remnant by God's electing grace has done so. Nevertheless, the rest were "blinded" or "hardened" The Greek word means to cover with a thick skin, to harden with a callous. As a metaphor it means to make the heart dull (see John 12:40). So the sense may apply to eyes, heart, or both.

Paul uses a combination of Deuteronomy 29:4 and Isaiah 29:10 (see Isa. 6:9–10) to support his statement. "Slumber" is the translation of the Greek word for insensibility of mind, a stupor, literally, "eyes of the not-to-see, and ears of the not-to-hear."

As in the case of Pharaoh (see 9:17), the question arises here as to who did this to Israel. The phrase "God gave" attributes it to God. However, to see him doing this arbitrarily is contrary to God's nature. The biblical record shows that Israel first adopted this attitude toward God's revelation. In time, after repeated refusals of God, God acted in accord with their own actions. Out of respect for man's free will God accepted as a fact what Israel had shown to be her attitude. As God gave Gentiles up to their chosen path, he did the same to Israel (see 1:24, 26, 28).

God works according to law. Psychologists say that when a person receives a stimulus but does not react favorably toward it, it goes away. It comes again but is not as strong as at the outset. Continued rejection finally results in no stimulus. This, in part, explains the meaning in the case at hand. We should not trifle with the approaches of God. Continued refusal leads to the condition where one cannot respond positively.

Paul's final example is a citation of Psalm 69:22–23 (vv. 9–10). Israel's unbelief became as a "snare" (net) used to catch birds and a hunter's "trap." "Table" suggests a feasting table. Israel continued to feast in her sense of false security, unaware that her unbelief in Christ was a snare and trap. She stumbled over Christ, and the exclusion of the mass of them was repayment for their hardness. "Recompence" is a just retribution. Blinded by their own unwillingness to see, they

bowed down in captivity to their hardened and senseless rebellion against God. The tragedy of the lost multitude of Jews
is made all the more evident by the remnant which believed/
believes unto salvation.

The Salvation of the Gentiles (11:11–24)

From discussing the failure of the Jews, Paul makes the
natural transition to the response of the Gentiles to the gospel.
"For it is the power of God unto salvation to every one that
believeth: to the Jew first, and also to the Greek" (1:16).
Whereas the Jews, other than the remnant, did not believe,
Gentiles in far greater numbers did believe, and salvation came
to those who believed. Israel was to be a priest-nation to Gentile
nations. The Old Testament taught that through Israel Gentiles
would also be brought to worship God (see Isa. 56:6–8). The
Suffering Servant is to bring justice and to be a "light of the
Gentiles" (see Isa. 42:1, 6). Israel was to be "for a light to
the Gentiles, that thou mayest be my salvation unto the end of
the earth" (Isa. 49:6). God chose Israel, not because he loved
her alone; but because he loves all people, he chose Israel. "For
all the earth is mine" (Exod. 19:5). It was through the faithful
remnant that Christ came, and he came to be Savior of the
entire world (see John 4:42).

Verses 11–12 are really transitional. Picking up the thought
in verse 9 Paul asks, "Have they [Israel] stumbled that they
should fall?" Robertson (p. 394) calls "should fall" (*pesōsin*
from *piptō*, to fall) an "effective aorist active subjunctive to
fall completely and for good." Is there no future hope for Israel? With his familiar "God forbid" Paul rejects this idea.
Indeed, the form of his question invites a negative answer.
Israel's temporary fall has resulted in salvation for the Gentiles.
Thus by Israel's failure or self-defeat, Gentiles have gained the
advantage once held by the Jews. It is not a complete cutting
off of the Jews but is designed to "provoke them to jealousy."
The verb so rendered is *parazēloō*, to burn with zeal alongside
(see 1 Cor. 10:22). Knox renders this "the result of that must
be to rouse the Jews to emulate them." The idea is to incite the
Jews so that they will desire the salvation which they have
spurned.

The Jews' fall has *diminished* their number who have received Christ. This has resulted in the "riches" of the Gentiles
—the large number of Gentiles who are saved. Paul, however,
still looks toward the "fulness" or full strength of their number
when they will turn to Christ.

Now Paul turns to speak directly to the Gentiles (v. 13). As the apostle to the Gentiles he magnifies his "ministry" (*diakonian*) as such. His address to the Gentiles is emphatic. "Now to you I am speaking, to the Gentiles." His magnifying his ministry is not for Gentiles only, but that he may also by winning them provoke to jealousy his brethren with respect to the flesh (Jews) and might save "some out of them" (literal). He does not see a saving of Jews as a whole or as a people.

If the casting away of the Jews resulted in the reconciling of the world (Gentiles) to God, the receiving again of Jews will be nothing less than "life from the dead" (v. 15). Some interpreters relate this to the idea that when the Jews are converted the end of the age will come. This, however, seems to go beyond Paul's meaning. He does not use the word *resurrection*. The sense seems to be that Jews turning to Christ will be as one rising from the dead. We need only to recall the difficulty in winning Jews to Christ today to catch his meaning.

Nevertheless, Paul does not give up hope (v. 16). "Firstfruit" and "root" do not refer to Jews already won to Christ. *Firstfruit* and *root* are parallels as are *lump* and *branches*. The figure of the firstfruit and lump refers to Numbers 15:17–21. When a portion of dough (firstfruit) was offered to the Lord, the entire lump was regarded as holy or dedicated to him. Changing his metaphor, Paul says that a holy root produces holy branches on the tree.

Some see "firstfruit" as referring to the patriarchs and "root" as related to Abraham. Since both are singular, it seems that in the context of Romans both refer to Abraham. The lump and branches refer to his descendants. Since Abraham was set apart for God's service (holy, position rather than character), so are his descendants set apart. However, we must keep in mind the distinction already drawn between natural and spiritual descendants of Abraham (see 4:13–16; 9:6–7). This is not a blanket promise to all Jews but to those who believe in Jesus Christ as Savior.

Paul continues the figure of root and branches through verse 24. Here he warns against Gentile pride. Some of the "branches" were broken off—natural Israel from spiritual Israel (v. 17). The "if" clause assumes this to be true. This provided room for the Gentiles to be grafted in. "And thou" (singular) shows that Paul now speaks to each individual Gentile Christian. Each one was a "wild olive" tree as opposed to the true olive tree of the true Israel. The olive tree is the most widely cultivated tree in the Middle East.

The ancients grafted wild olive branches into an old tree in

order to invigorate the latter. Noting this custom, Robertson
(p. 396) says, however, that the wild branch did not produce as
good fruit as the original. This point should not be pressed here.
The apostle is simply using a common practice to show God's
purpose for the Gentiles. In verse 24 he clearly shows that this
is contrary to nature. Also in verse 17 he shows how the graft
shares in the life of the root—in this case the spiritual heritage
of Abraham.

In verse 18 Paul begins his warning to the Gentile Christians: "Boast [glory] not against the branches." This may well
read, "Stop boasting" or "Do not have the habit of boasting."
Gentiles should remember that "thou bearest not the root, but
the root thee." Both "thou" and "thee" are emphatic. The branch
feeds upon the root; the branch does not feed the root. The
Gentile Christians receive spiritual strength as true seed of
Abraham, but they do not give the same to him.

Paul imagines a claim from Gentile Christians that they
have replaced the Jews as God's people (v. 19). This evidently
was an element of their pride. "Well" (v. 20) translates *kalōs*.
Ordinarily this word carries the idea of the good and beautiful.
However, here Paul probably used it as irony (Denney, p. 680).
It could mean, "Well, what you say is true up to a point," but
Paul hastens to show the other side of the coin. What happened
to Israel was due to her unbelief. The Gentile Christians are
established in their present position through faith. But rather
than being proud, the Gentile Christians should see the Jewish
experience as a warning. The Jews as natural branches seemingly had a more secure position with God than the Gentiles
as grafted-in branches (v. 21). If God did not spare unbelieving
Jews, he also was able not to spare the Gentiles. It is clear here
that Paul is talking to unsaved Gentiles as a group, not to an
individual Gentile Christian who is already saved (see Denney,
p. 681; Wuest, pp. 196–97). The branches that were cut off
were unbelieving Israelites. Thus they were not saved or fit for
use in God's redemptive purpose. Paul is thinking of the same
situation among Gentiles.

In verse 22 Paul contrasts God's "goodness and severity"—
goodness toward those who believe; severity toward those who
do not believe. We must see this verse in terms of the body of
Jews and the body of Gentiles. When it became evident that the
Jews would not fulfill their covenant as a priest-nation, they
were cut off from it. Should the Gentiles prove likewise, the
same will be their lot. Denney says, "It is not to Israel only God
may say, The kingdom is taken from you, and given to a nation
bringing forth the fruits thereof" (p. 681). This should serve

as a warning to every Christian body today. None has a peculiar claim on God. When a given group refuses to be used of God, he chooses another. God does not need us as much as we need him.

The apostle holds out hope for the Jews if they return to God in faith (v. 23). If God cut them off because of unbelief, he certainly can graft them in again on the basis of their faith. This he proves by a reference to Gentiles who were cut off a wild olive tree and grafted into the domestic tree. He surely can take the natural branches and graft them into "their own olive tree" (v. 24).

Some interpreters object to Paul's figure of the wild olive branches being grafted into a domestic tree, but he himself notes that it is "contrary to nature." However, "God is able" flavors this entire figure. God is able to do by grace what is impossible by law. This very fact of "contrary to nature" removes any grounds for Gentile pride over the Jew. The true people of God are both Jews and Gentiles who receive Christ as Savior.

The Mystery of Israel (11:25–32)

The word *mystery* was used in the mystery religions of Paul's day to refer to secret knowledge available only to the members of a given religion. Paul adopted the word and gave it a Christian meaning. To him it is something which cannot be discovered through human reason but must be received by divine revelation. For the most part Paul used it of God's purpose in Christ and the church (see Rom. 16:25; 1 Cor. 2:7; 15:51; Eph. 3:3–4, 9; Col. 1:26–27; 2:2). In Romans 11:25 he uses it of the mystery of Israel.

Paul does not want the Gentiles, out of ignorance of this mystery, to be wise in themselves (*en heautois*). This has reference to Gentile pride. Whereas Pharaoh's heart was fully hardened, Israel is only partially blinded. This will continue "until the fulness of the Gentiles be come in" (v. 25). In Romans 11:12 Paul spoke of the fullness of the Jews. There "fulness" was seen as the full strength or number of Jews to be saved eventually. In verse 25 the same idea is used of Gentiles. Some see "fulness" as referring to both Jews and Gentiles simultaneously. However, in the context (vv. 12, 25) the fullness of the Jews follows that of the Gentiles.

However, "fulness" should not be seen as referring to a predetermined number of Gentiles to be saved, and then a predetermined number of Jews who will also be saved. The idea is more that as the Gentiles come to Christ in full strength, this fact will provoke the Jews to jealousy so that they will turn to Christ. We cannot repeat too often and strongly that this does not teach a mass turning of Jews to Christ or a saving *en masse*. Not all Jews will be saved, even as not all Gentiles will be saved. God has one plan of salvation for both. Peter, the apostle to the Jews, stated it in Acts 15:11: "But we believe that through the grace of the Lord Jesus ["Christ" not in best manuscripts] we [Jews] shall be saved, even as they [Gentiles]." Only those Jews and Gentiles who receive Christ as Savior will be saved. And it must be on an individual basis.

I was once in a workshop of chaplains and pastors near a military base. The post chaplain was a Jewish rabbi, who presided at the meetings. Around the lunch table a discussion was held. A pastor asked the rabbi about efforts by conservative rabbis in Israel to ban all Christian missionary work. Denying that this would be done, the rabbi said, "In Israeli schools it is required that all children study the life of Jesus. Notice that I said 'Jesus,' not 'Christ.'" I could not help but hope, thinking what the Holy Spirit could do in using this *history* to a spiritual advantage in leading many or all of these children to trust in *Christ* as Savior. We can only hope and pray.

"And so all Israel shall be saved" (v. 26). To support this statement Paul combines quotations from Isaiah 59:20–21 and 27:9 (vv. 26–27). The question here is as to the meaning of "all Israel." Some interpreters see this as including all Jewish people. Others, in the line of Origen, see this as universalism, or that all Jews and Gentiles will be saved. However, neither of these positions agrees with the larger context of Romans—or the New Testament as a whole. Moody (p. 245) refers to those who see it in terms of the salvation of Israel as "a collective conversion" that does not include every Israelite. Noting the difficulty in finding a solution, he adds that "this seems to be the best solution." "Collective conversion" is not clear. If it means a mass saving of certain Jews, that is one thing. If it means that in a comparatively brief period many Jews will turn to Jesus Christ in faith, that is another thing. With the latter idea I agree, but it will be individual salvation resulting from individual faith.

However, to me the most logical solution seems to lie in the idea that "Israel" in verse 26 includes both Jews and Gentiles who have believed in Jesus as Lord. In Romans 9:6 Paul distinguishes between Israel as a corporate people and the Israel of faith. The true seed of Abraham are his by faith, including both believing Jews and Gentiles (see 1 Pet. 2:1–10); so "all

Israel" is made up of all who believe in Jesus as Savior. It is the true, the spiritual Israel of God—composed of the believing remnant of Jews and also Gentiles who believe. This does not rule out a large turning of Jews to Christ at some future time, but it includes the "fulness" of both Jews and Gentiles (see 11:12, 25). Thus "all Israel shall be saved" by grace through faith in Christ, but they are saved as individuals.

This position seems to be supported by verses 28–32. The rebellion of Israel opened the way for Gentiles to hear the gospel and to be saved. However, God's election for believing Jews will not be recalled or regretted. Gentiles who, in past time, were *disobedient* (true reading, not "believed") have obtained mercy because of the *disobedience* (unbelief) of Israel. The Jews continue in disobedience, but provoked to jealousy by the saved Gentiles, they will obey the gospel and be saved.

"For God hath concluded them all [Jews and Gentiles] in unbelief [disobedience], that he might have mercy upon all" (v. 32). "Mercy upon all" means that disobedient Jews and Gentiles alike *may* receive God's mercy, but it does not mean that they *shall* do so. It depends upon each person's response to the gospel. Moody is right when he says that "it is universal invitation but not universal salvation that is taught" (p. 246).

The Wisdom of God (11:33–36)

Paul's carefully reasoned discussion of God's redemptive purpose as it pertains to both Jews and Gentiles has brought him to the heights. Standing upon the summit of the mighty mountain he has scaled, he views the panorama of God's electing grace and love. Realizing that try as he will he cannot plumb the depths of the riches of God's wisdom and knowledge, he bursts forth in a hymn of praise (see Moody, p. 247, for an analysis of it).

"O the depth of the riches both of the wisdom and knowledge of God! how unsearchable are his judgments, and his ways past finding out!" (v. 33). We can know some things about God, but it is like dipping water out of the ocean with a spoon. "Riches" suggests the inexhaustible supply of love, grace, and spiritual resources which are revealed in Christ. Mere man cannot hope to comprehend God's inscrutable decisions. The Greek word translated "past finding out" means to trace something to its source. No one can trace to their source God's ways of dealing with men; the trail runs out before reaching it (see Eph. 3:8; Job 5:9; 9:10).

"For who hath known the mind of the Lord? or who hath

been his counsellor? Or who hath first given to him, and it shall be recompensed unto him again?" (vv. 34–35). Verse 34 is a quotation of Isaiah 40:13 (see 1 Cor. 2:16). Verse 35 seems to be the apostle's own translation of Job 41:11 (Robertson, p. 400). The idea is who can purchase God's favor since he owns all.

Literally, "Because out of him [source], and through him [agent], and unto him [goal] are all things [*ta panta*, the universe as a whole]" (v. 36; see Col. 1:16). Paul can only conclude: "To him the glory unto the ages [or forever]. Amen!"

11

The Practical Exhortation

Romans 12:1–15:33

Paul was a master logician and theologian. His carefully reasoned development of the gospel is one of the greatest applications of logic in all literature. The apostle was/is without parallel as a theological thinker. But at the same time he never divorced belief from behavior. Christian faith not only should result in Christian living, but Paul, like James (see James 2), held that one should prove his faith by his works.

Therefore, in Romans he followed his usual pattern of expounding and then applying the doctrine. This application is found in chapters 12–15. Chapter 12 deals with the Christian life as one of sacrifice. Chapter 13 relates the Christian life to public duty. Romans 14:1–15:7 treats Christian relationships. Romans 15:8–14 relates Christ's ministry to the problem of fellowship in Rome. The remainder of chapter 15 deals with Paul's ministry itself.

The Living Sacrifice (12:1–2)

Paul's readers have been redeemed by the once-for-all sacrifice of Christ; so he calls upon them to live the sacrificial life for Christ.

"I beseech you therefore, brethren, by the mercies of God, that ye present your bodies a living sacrifice, holy, acceptable unto God, which is your reasonable service" (v. 1).

"Therefore" refers to all that Paul has said in chapters 1–11. On this basis he makes his appeal. The emphatic word is "beseech" (*parakalō*) since it comes first in the verse. Basically the word means to call alongside. Paul calls his readers alongside himself in living the sacrificial life. However, this verb may also mean to exhort or encourage. "Exhort" is the more natural meaning here. It expresses a strong "appeal" (RSV). "Brethren," used here in the Christian sense, suggests the fellowship in which the readers are to respond. Paul's appeal is based upon the "mercies" or compassion which God has shown in Christ.

147

According to Josephus (*Antiquities* IV. 6.4) the Greek verb translated "present" (literally, to stand alongside) was used of offering a sacrifice. In contrast to the dead bodies in animal sacrifice, they should offer their *bodies* as living sacrifices (see 1 Cor. 6:19–20; "And in your spirit, which are God's" is not in the best texts of 1 Corinthians 6:20). We are so to dedicate our bodies as to glory God. "Holy" means set apart for God's service. Of course, such bodies should be clean and pure. Such will be "acceptable" or well-pleasing to God. The body is not inherently evil, but it should be dedicated to God if it is to fulfill its purpose. The word translated "reasonable" means "rational" as distinguished from the material. It is reasonable that a redeemed body should be used for God's service. However, in this context "spiritual" is more likely Paul's meaning. As rational it refers to the inner man. The Greek word translated "service" refers to a service of worship (see 9:4). Dedicated service to and for God is worship of God.

In verse 2 Paul shows, first negatively and then positively, how to do this. Literally, "Stop being conformed to this world," or "age." The Greek word *aiōn*, "age," connotes a social order that takes no note of God or his will. Wuest (p. 207) quotes Trench to the effect that the word connotes "all that floating mass of thoughts, opinions, maxims, speculations, hopes, impulses, aims, aspirations" which constitute the worldly atmosphere in which we live. "Conformed" means to be fashioned according to another's pattern. It denotes the idea of appearing to be on the outside what one really is not on the inside. In this case it refers to Christians whose outward lives bely their inner confession as children of God. It is like masquerading as a person of the world rather than living as a child of God. In the passive voice, as here, it means that the age is doing this to the Christian.

"Be ye transformed" is the positive side of the coin. The Greek verb *metamorphoō* is the one from which comes the English "metamorphosis." It means to change your outward appearance so as to agree with your inner self. In the case of a Christian it is to let your outward appearance and conduct be in keeping with your inner Christian nature. This verb is used of Jesus' transfiguration (see Matt. 17:2). His deity shone forth from within so that it was evident in his outward appearance. The passive voice here also means that this is done to the Christian by someone else—the Holy Spirit. So you are either being conformed by this evil age or being transformed by the Holy Spirit. Of course, in either case the cooperation of the person involved is a part of the process.

The Holy Spirit transforms you "by the renewing of your mind," or by making new again your mind or total inner self. From what you were before becoming a Christian, you must be changed into that which God envisions for all his children. This renewing of the mind suggests first repentance—a change of heart, mind, and attitude—but it extends beyond that to a gradual transformation into the new spiritual relationship which you have assumed in Christ. It will not be accomplished in a day, but we should be on our way toward the goal (see Gal. 5:16; 2 Pet. 3:18). In the reference in 2 Peter "grow" means "go on growing" or do it habitually.

The purpose or goal of the process is expressed by *eis* (toward, as a goal) and an infinitive of purpose (*dokimazein*). This present infinitive means to go on proving by testing with respect to oneself "what God's will is—the good, and acceptable [well-pleasing] and perfect [complete]" will. The idea is so to test God's will as to find it meeting all specifications for your Christian life and to place your approval upon it.

The Church: Christ's Body (12:3–8)

In this section Paul views his readers as members of a body which he identifies as the body of Christ (see 12:5). This is a favorite figure of Paul in describing the relationship of Christians to Christ and to each other (see 1 Cor. 12; Eph. 1:22–23; 4:12–16; Col. 1:18). So growing out of his appeal in Romans 12:1–2 are his words as to how Christians should live in this intimate relationship.

"For" (v. 3) shows that the following is the natural outcome of full surrender to God's will. The "grace" given to Paul could refer to Paul's office as an apostle which was a gift of God's grace. Some see him as using himself as a pattern for his readers to follow. Both could be involved. If so, the former involves *authority*, and the latter means *example*. The advice he gives was/is needed by every Christian.

In this verse there is a play on the Greek word *phronein*, to think. One should not "overthink" (*huperphronein*) beyond what he should "think" (*phronein*) but "think" (*phronein*) "soberly" (*sōphronein*) or sanely. Paul considers *overthinking* or *high-thinking* as a kind of insanity. The body of Christ should be a sane body. This could be a reference to the pride of Gentile Christians in their regard for Jews (see 11:18–19). While this may be true, as the account develops it is related to the relative importance of individual Christians and their spiritual gifts to be used in God's service. Since Romans was written from Corinth, this could reflect the problem treated in 1 Corinthians 12–13. "To every man" is emphatic in the Greek text. So to each one God has divided the measure of faith. Each one has his gift from God; so there is no basis for individual pride (see 1 Cor. 4:7; 12:4–11). The human body has many members, each with a different practice or function (v. 4). "So we, being many, are one body in Christ, and every one members one of another" (v. 5). Each Christian has his own particular gift to be used in the Lord's service. When all function properly, the *body* is healthy and efficient. "Members one of another" shows the close relationship of those who are in Christ. This does not mean that we cease to be individual personalities but that we bear a mutual relationship within the body of Christ. In the human body the heart does not cease to be the heart, but its function and well-being are related to other organs of the body. The analogy applies in the spiritual body of Christ.

Each part of this body should function efficiently according to its nature and intent but in harmony with other parts, for each part complements the others. This Paul shows in verses 6–8. If one's gift be prophecy, he should exercise it "according to the proportion of faith." "Faith" here is subjective, the faith in the person. This means that one should declare clearly God's revelation with fervor and strength in keeping with his proportion of faith. Even in the Old Testament, while prophets foretold the future, their major role was to tell forth God's message to their own generation. This is even more so the case in the New Testament. There a prophet was one who could preach the gospel with great power. Such an ability should not be a source of pride but a means of service.

Since "according to the proportion of faith" occurs only once, followed by a series of other services, it should be read with all of them. "Ministry" (*diakonian*) involves the broad aspect of serving, including the most menial kind. "Teaching" means just that. "Exhorteth" here probably should be read as encouragement or comfort. Giving, helping those in need, should be done simply or without a public show. Ruling means one standing in front, a leader. "Diligence" means haste or to lead in earnestness. One is not ready to lead until he is willing to follow. "Mercy" (visiting the sick, sorrowful, and poor?) should be shown "with cheerfulness"—brightness and a joyful attitude. One should carry sunshine, not gloom, to those in need.

These are but samples of the functions of the parts of Christ's body, but they furnish a guide for all other parts. Christ ministers to others through his people. To serve others in his name is to serve him.

The Church: a Fellowship (12:9–21)

The church, whether local or general, is not only a body with reference to Christ, it is also a fellowship with reference to those making up the fellowship. The New Testament never refers to church *membership* but to church *fellowship,* which means having all things in common or a sharing of both privileges and responsibilities. This fellowship is effected through the Holy Spirit (see 1 Cor. 12:13). For this fellowship to be real and wholesome, there must be a unity of attitude and purpose.

"Love" (v. 9) is the highest kind of love (*agapē*). It characterizes God's nature (see 1 John 4:8) and is our response to his love as we love him and other Christians (see 1 John 4:7–21). W. Hersey Davis once described *agapē* as absolute loyalty to its object (see Rom. 5:8). He said the one English word which best translates it is *selflessness.* This selflessness should be shown without "dissimulation" or "hypocrisy" (*anupokritos*). It should not be hypocritical, play-acting, pretended love, but a genuine expression of it (v. 9). We are to "abhor" or intensely dislike the evil, and "cleave to," or prefer, the good. "With brotherly love [*philadelphia*] toward one another be tenderly affectioned" (v. 10, literal). "Tenderly affectioned" translates an adjective used of the mutual love of parent and child. Rather than to be self-seeking, in honor prefer one another. Boost others rather than yourself.

The Greek word translated "business" means one's vocation (v. 11). One should not be "slow and 'pokey'" (Robertson, p. 404). "Fervent" translates a Greek word meaning "boiling" (zealous). So we should be zealous in the sphere of the Holy Spirit as we serve the Lord as his slaves. The definite article in the Greek text shows that the Holy Spirit is Paul's meaning. This boiling zeal is in the life produced by the Spirit.

"Rejoicing in [the] hope" (v. 12) means in the sphere of hope. "The hope" refers to the hope that they have in Christ, so "your hope" (RSV; see 8:24–25). Such rejoicing gives patient endurance in time of trial. The secret to such patience is perseverance in prayer. "Distributing" translates the Greek verb *koinōneō* from which comes *koinonia,* "fellowship"; so it means a sharing with Christians in need. This thought following "instant in prayer" suggests Acts 6:1–4 (see Gal. 2:10). "Hospitality" translates a Greek word meaning "love for strangers."

Their homes should be open to traveling Christians. Public accommodations at their best were not too good then.

Verse 14 reads like words of Jesus. Christians not only live in a blessed fellowship but in a hostile world. When persecuted by the enemies of Christ and the gospel, they should not return evil for evil but good for evil. The Greek word for "bless" is *eulogeō*, to speak well or to eulogize. "Curse not" means not to have the habit of calling down divine curses on those persecuting you.

Verse 15 uses two absolute infinitives as finite verbs, literally, "Rejoicing with rejoicing people, weeping with weeping people"; that is, to share with others in whatever state they are in. To be of one mind is "thinking the same thing with respect to one another" (v. 16). "Mind" could also read "spirit." Paul is not thinking of uniformity but unanimity of spirit which is necessary in a harmonious fellowship. The negatives in the remainder of this verse explain the unanimity. Literally, "Stop thinking the high things." This does not mean to avoid noble thoughts but to avoid haughtiness (RSV). Instead the Christian should "condescend to men of low estate." "Men of low estate" can be either masculine or neuter in gender; so it may refer to men or things. "Condescend" translates a passive form of the Greek verb which means to lead away together. One should not be conceited but should be willing to identify with humble people or to do the humble task.

Christians should not pay back evil done to them by doing evil to the evildoer (v. 17). "Provide" should read "take thought beforehand." They should plan ahead with respect to the good before all men. We should act in accord with our inner Christian spirit. This means that one is honest in his behavior, as his outward expression toward others is in accord with his true self.

If possible, the Christian should be at peace with all men (v. 18). Some people will not let you live peaceably with them. "As much as lieth in you" translates "the things out of you." The cause of strife should never originate with the Christian.

Furthermore, Christians should not "avenge themselves," or exact justice from others for wrongs done to them (v. 19). The tense in the Greek suggests that they were doing it and should stop. They should not take the law into their own hands. "The wrath" is God's wrath; so it should be given its rightful place. "Vengeance" rightfully belongs to God (see Deut. 32:35). God says that he will pay back to the evildoer for his evil. God's vengeance is not retaliatory in nature. It is the law of his "wrath" (*orgē*, see 1:18) in operation. Further, to support his words Paul quotes Proverbs 25:21-22 (v. 20).

The Christian should not be conquered (*nikō*) by evil but should conquer evil with good or in the sphere of the good (v. 21). To strike back with evil for evil only feeds the flames of evil. Robertson (p. 406) says, "Drown the evil in the good." This will work, not only in the church fellowship, but in the Christian's relationship with the world outside.

The Christian and Citizenship (13:1-7)

The Christian is a citizen of two *kingdoms,* the kingdom of God and the earthly nation of which he is a part, and he is to be a good citizen of both. Christianity was born in an empire of tyranny. It has lived under every type of government. While the believer may not agree with the governmental philosophy or policies of his nation, he is to be a good citizen of it. So long as a law does not violate his conscience before God, the Christian should obey it. Even if he defies such a law, he should be prepared and willing to endure the consequences of his allegiance to God.

"Let every soul [person] be subject unto the higher powers. For there is no power but of God: the powers that be are ordained of God" (v. 1). "Be subject" translates the Greek verb which means to be lined up in order as troops under a commander. Some see "higher powers" as invisible powers or fallen angels now subjected to God. However, the context here seems to call for governmental powers over the people. All such power comes from God or does not exist "except by God." This does not mean that God is responsible for evil rulers or for the evil acts of nations but that God has established the institution of government to insure an orderly society. Nor does it rule out a change in form of government, even by revolution when the majority of people deem a government impossible. Where possible, of course, it is better to change a government's role through due process. Primarily Paul is talking about obedience to law. Lawlessness is against God. Such must expect to receive "judgment" (*krima*) by the state and eventually by God (v. 2). Not law-abiding people but criminals need fear those having the rule (v. 3). Legal authority is designed to protect the innocent (good citizens) who shall receive the praise of the government. Peter says that even if Christians suffer by disobedience to laws which violate their consciences they should suffer as Christians and not as criminals (1 Pet. 4:14-16).

Note that in verse 4 Paul calls a ruler a "minister" (*diakonos,* deacon) of God, a term usually applied to Christians. But wherever God's will is involved, his instrument is a *diakonos.* He is a minister for good to law-abiding people. Even a Christian who breaks the law has a reason to fear the authorities. To a law-abiding citizen a policeman is a source of protection. To those who break the law he is a source of justice for society. "Beareth not the sword in vain" suggests two things. Law officers wore a sword as a modern policeman wears a gun or club, but the sword was also used for capital punishment involving Roman citizens. It seems that both ideas may apply here.

Now a Christian should not obey the law merely out of fear of punishment (v. 5). He is subject to the higher law of Christian conscience. Thus one should not obey the law only when an officer is near. He should do so out of a Christian conscience as a duty to God. His controlling power should not be external force but inner compulsion.

Verses 6–7 teach the payment of various taxes to support the services rendered by the government. "Tribute" means that which is brought or taxes. The Greek word translated "ministers" in verse 6 is *leitourgos.* It was used of anyone who rendered public service, a servant of the state. It also was used of the service of priests in the temple. So one is a minister of God whether he leads in worship or enforces the law. Both the temple (church) and the state are God's institutions.

"Dues" (v. 7) means the things which are owed. Christians have a moral obligation to honor debts whether to a merchant or to the state. For "tribute" see verse 6. "Custom" was an indirect tax on goods which one bought. Robertson (p. 408) notes that "tribute" (*phoros*) was a tax paid to a nation which subjected another. *Telos* was a tax to support civil government. "Fear" (respect) and "honour" should be directed toward those whose due it is to receive such. Even if one does not respect the person occupying an office (for example, Nero), one should respect and honor the office. This is a much-needed admonition today.

The Christian as a Neighbor (13:8–10)

Every Christian is a neighbor (one who dwells beside) to others, and he should be a good neighbor both to the saved and unsaved.

One may pay his taxes in full, but the demands of Christian love (*agapē*) can never be fully paid; so the Christian is obligated to love his neighbor (v. 8). Origen said, "The debt of love remains with us permanently and never leaves us; this is a debt which we both discharge every day, but forever owe." Robertson says, "This debt can never be paid off, but we should keep the interest paid up" (p. 409).

Such love is a fulfillment of the Mosaic law (see v. 9). Note that Paul cites only those laws which deal with our obligations to other people. One must first love God absolutely (see Exod. 19:3–11, first four commandments) and then "love thy neighbour as thyself" (see last six of the Ten Commandments; see also Lev. 19:18). In the parable of the Good Samaritan (Luke 10:25–37) Jesus shows that my neighbor is anyone in need— regardless of where he lives. Modern communications and travel have made the world a neighborhood. Since love works no ill to one's neighbor, it fulfills the law (v. 10). More than anything else the modern world needs Christian *neighbors!*

The Christian and Crisis (13:11–14)

Moody (p. 261) calls this passage a "Hymn of the Day of Christ." Throughout his treatment of Romans he points to certain passages here and elsewhere as *hymns* sung in the early church. Laughingly he told me recently that his colleagues in Southern Baptist Theological Seminary kidded him by saying that before he finished he would turn the entire New Testament into a hymn book! There is a large school of thought along this line. My purpose, however, hymn or not, is to show what Paul is saying. However one labels this passage, Paul is dealing with Christian conduct in the light of the crisis of the age—the return of the Lord.

"And that, knowing the time, that now it is high time to awake out of sleep: for now is our salvation nearer than when we believed" (v. 11).

"Knowing" means perceptive, full knowledge. "Time" (*kairos*) refers to the crisis-time of the Lord's return. "High time" renders *hōra*, like our "hour." The hour to awake from sleep has arrived. Paul's figure is that of the dawn of a new day—the Lord's return, for now our "salvation" is nearer than when we believed in Christ. The mere passing of time would make this true. Every passing day makes this the case. However, the use of *kairos* (time) points to an opportune crisis event. "Salvation" here means final, full salvation ending in glorification (see Heb. 9:28).

Continuing the idea of night and day, Paul says that the night is coming to an end; so it is time to put off our night

clothes and put on our "armour" or tools (*hopla*) of light, or
that worn in the daytime (v. 12). We should "walk," or live,
honorably as befits daytime living (v. 13). Paul uses *walk*
thirty-three times in the sense of living. We *talk* as we *walk*.
This is contrasted with the works of darkness or things done
at night (v. 13). Paul closes this with an exhortation to be
clothed in the Lord Jesus Christ (v. 14). By contrast his readers
are to stop doing the things of the flesh planned beforehand
with respect to evil desires. All these things (vv. 13–14) the
Christian should do in daily expectancy of the Lord's return.
We should do nothing that we would not want to be found doing when he comes. Rather we should be found living for him
(see Matt. 24:45–51). Even if he delays his return, he is with
us every moment in his Spirit. This should be an incentive to
holy living.

Did Paul expect the Lord to return in his lifetime? While he
entertained the possibility of his death prior to that time (see
2 Cor. 5:1–9), the greater emphasis was upon his being alive
when that event took place (see 1 Cor. 15:51–57; 1 Thess.
4:17). Some generation will be alive when Jesus returns. Paul's
was the only living generation then; so he was doing exactly
what Jesus told his people to do, to be alert and ready when he
comes (see Matt. 24:36, 42, 44). Every Christian should live
on tiptoe in faith "looking for that blessed hope, and the glorious appearing of the great God and [even] our Saviour Jesus
Christ" (Titus 2:13).

The Christian and Christian Relationships (14:1–15:7)

This passage about Jewish dietary laws reads much like
1 Corinthians 8–10. There, along with other matters, Paul
dealt with the conflict between two groups over whether or not
to eat meat offered to idols. This is significant since Romans
was written from Corinth. Galatians, probably also written
from Corinth, reflects the problem of observing days and sea-
sons (see Gal. 4:8–11). This is also a problem here (see Rom.
14:5–6). Apparently the problems which plagued the church
in Corinth were also present in Rome. The discussion in both
letters reflects a strong majority and a weak minority. The
strong felt that freedom in Christ overruled Jewish dietary
laws, but the weak felt differently. This dispute also reflects a
large Gentile majority as over against a Jewish minority.

Evidently the majority wished to exclude the minority (v. 1).
Paul says to "take to yourselves" the weak, but not for the
purpose of debate. The strong felt that they could eat meat

offered to idols without worshiping the idol (v. 2). The weak, feeling otherwise, had become vegetarians. Neither group should despise or set at nought the other. For God has received both on the basis of faith (v. 3). To illustrate his point Paul uses a brief parable. One should not judge another's house servant (v. 4). He stands or falls before his own owner or lord. Likewise, the "Lord" (best texts) is able to make his own to stand. Judgment should be left with the Lord, not each one judging his Christian brother (see 12:19).

Another problem was related to what day one should reserve for worship (vv. 5–6). This reflects the transition from the seventh to the first day of the week. Evidently the Jewish minority held on to the Sabbath, whereas the Gentile majority observed the Lord's day. Paul does not arbitrarily settle the matter. "Let every man be fully persuaded in his own mind" (v. 5). Though he favored the majority position (15:1; see Acts 20:7; 1 Cor. 16:2), he was patient with the minority. Whether it be with regard to food or the day of worship, it should be observed as unto the Lord or in his honor (v. 6). Robertson (p. 413) notes "Paul's principle of freedom in non-essentials." Liberty in Christ should not lead one group to force its position upon another. Paul could be very obstinate where the basic principles of the gospel were concerned (see Gal. 1:6–9), but he could be tolerant of another's spirit as long as he preached Christ (see Phil. 1:14–18).

Regardless of one's personal position, we all live and/or die "unto the Lord" (vv. 7–8). His death and resurrection confirm that he is Lord over all (v. 9). We are to leave judgment of one another to him (v. 10). As Paul had stood before the *bēma* (judgment seat) of Gallio (see Acts 18:12), so all men must appear before the *bēma* of Christ. "So then every one of us shall give account of himself to God" (v. 12). Note "of himself," not of the conduct of others. We have enough to consider in ourselves without throwing stumblingblocks in the path of others (v. 13). I have enough trouble keeping myself straight!

Though Paul is thoroughly convinced ("I know perceptively and am fully persuaded," both verbs are perfect tenses) "in the sphere of the Lord Jesus" (not by rational processes) that nothing is unclean in itself, some do not so regard it (v. 14, literal). To them unclean meat is unclean. For the latter to eat such meat becomes sin for them. Therefore, Paul admonishes the strong to respect the dietary scruples of the weak (v. 15). Seeing the strong eating meat, the weak regard them as idolaters. If the former persuades the weak to act contrary to their consciences, they cause them to sin and also sin against them.

So he pleads for Christian love, not knowledge, to be the guiding principle. "Not charitably" means "not according to love" (*agapē*). "Destroy not him with thy meat, for whom Christ died" (v. 15; see 1 Cor. 8:9–13).

Even though there is nothing wrong with the Christian eating this meat, one should not let his "good be evil spoken of" by weak Christians (v. 16). The kingdom of God is more than what one eats or drinks. It is "righteousness, and peace, and joy in the Holy Ghost [Spirit]" (v. 17). For the latter a Christian should be willing to forego the former. "These things" in verse 18 refers to the spiritual virtues in verse 17. All Christians should follow after these to build up one another (v. 19). The Greek verb translated "destroy" (v. 20) may read "loosen down" or undermine as the foundation of a building. This agrees with "edify" in verse 19. Things that may not be wrong within themselves are wrong if they provide a snare to trap others or lead them to sin (v. 21). Regardless of what one's faith teaches him, it should be practiced before God and with due regard for others (v. 22), but the weak brother who eats meat contrary to his conscience is condemned, or judged down, for his act (v. 23). He is guilty of sin because whatever one does contrary to his Christian faith is sin.

Romans 15:1 reads, literally, "We the strong are under obligation to bear the weaknesses of the not strong." Note the emphasis upon "we" and that Paul identifies himself with the majority. The strong should act so as to please his neighbor, not to gain his favor, but to edify him (v. 2). Even "the Christ" (Greek text, "the Messiah") did not please himself as shown in Psalm 69:9 (v. 3). This was regarded as a messianic psalm. Hence "the Christ" rather than "Christ" as a proper name. The Scriptures were written for our instruction, wherein the Christian rests his hope (v. 4). The Greek word for "hope" may be translated "exhortation," "encouragement," or "comfort." Verses 5–6 form a prayer that God may grant that Paul's readers may be like-minded toward one another according to the character and example of Christ. This will restore the harmony which was disturbed, as is shown in chapter 14. Verse 7 is directed to both the strong and the weak Christians.

The Ministry of Christ (15:8–14)

Since the disturbance in the church fellowship involved Jews and Gentiles, Paul reminds them of Christ's ministry to both (vv. 8–9). He establishes this fact with a series of Scripture quotations: verse 9 (Ps. 18:49); verse 10 (Deut. 32:43);

verse 11 (Ps. 117:1); verse 12 (Isa. 11:10). Moody (p. 273) quotes Hunter to the effect that whereas 3:10–18 teaches "the universality of sin," these passages teach "the universality of salvation"—not *universalism* but *universality.*

In verse 13 Paul again prays that the God of hope will fill his believing readers with joy and peace, that they may "abound" or overflow in the sphere of hope by the Holy Spirit's power. He himself is fully confident that they also are filled with goodness and Christian knowledge as he is, so that they are able to admonish one another (v. 14). They can settle their differences in the spirit of Christ who is the center of their faith. As he has redeemed them, so he can guide them through the Holy Spirit. The centrality of this church is such in the western Mediterranean region that they can set the example for others. And like Thessalonica in the east, they can be a sounding board of the gospel for that entire area (see 1 Thess. 1:8).

The Ministry of Paul (15:15–33)

Paul, of course, was the apostle to the Gentiles (see Acts 9:15; 13:2; Gal. 2:7). It is as such that he has written this letter "more boldly" in which he has said some rather sharp things. "The grace" given to him of God is this Gentile ministry (vv. 15–16). Note that even though he is an apostle, he also calls himself a priest. "Minister" translates the Greek word *leitourgos* which was used of a priest in the Jerusalem temple. So he is also "a priest of Jesus Christ to the Gentiles." This places him in the priestly succession. "Ministering" means to serve as a priest in the gospel of God. As such he places his offering of the Gentile body of Christianity before God as one being sanctified in the Holy Spirit in order that it may be acceptable to God. He has that in which he may glory through Jesus Christ "in those things which pertain to God" (v. 17). This was a phrase used in Jewish liturgical language to refer to functions of worship (see Heb. 2:17; 5:1).

Paul refuses to speak of anything except those which Christ has wrought through him (v. 18), but Christ's work through him in word and deed has been to the end that Gentiles might be obedient to the Lord. "Mighty signs and wonders" speaks of miracles. "Mighty" renders a form of the word *dunamis*, power; signs (*sēmeiōn*) and "wonders," works causing people to wonder or take notice (*teratōn*), form the usual combination used for miracles. These were wrought in the power of the Holy Spirit.

The result is "that from Jerusalem, and round about unto

Illyricum, I have fully preached the gospel of Christ" (v. 19). Of course, Paul's first preaching of the gospel was in Damascus, and later in Jerusalem. The word *round* means "in a ring." So after his beginning in Damascus, Jerusalem, and Antioch where churches already existed, Paul had established a *ring* of churches about the northern half of the eastern Mediterranean reaching to Illyricum. This province was on the northwestern edge of the Grecian peninsula, bordering on the Adriatic Sea. No record exists of this ministry in Illyricum. It occurred probably while he waited for word from Corinth as to the effect the Corinthian letters had had on the church there (see Robertson, p. 421; Acts 20:1-3; 2 Cor. 13). Paul's use of "Jerusalem . . . Illyricum" suggests Acts 1:8. It seems that Paul wanted to carry out this commission literally (see v. 24).

As an apostle Paul was a pioneer, a missionary (see Eph. 4:11). He did not wish to build upon another's foundation but to evangelize where Christ's name had not been heard (v. 20). Verse 21 quotes Isaiah 52:15 as scriptural support for this plan. Because of this Paul has been hindered, or cut off, from visiting Rome (v. 22), but now that he has planted the gospel throughout the above-mentioned area, he plans to visit the church in Rome on his way to Spain, more pioneer territory (vv. 23-24). He does not plan a long stay in Rome simply to build upon a foundation already laid. Virgin territory awaits him in Spain, which to the Roman world was "the uttermost part of the earth" (Acts 1:8). Until the time of Columbus the ancients had a saying about Spain as "Ne Plus Ultra," no more beyond. After the discovery of America the "Ne" was dropped.

In addition to Spain's being "the uttermost part of the earth," Barclay notes that "at this time Spain was experiencing a kind of blaze of genius" (p. 204). He mentions the great men of the empire who came from there. This, plus the fact of many Jews with their synagogues being there, made Spain a fruitful area in which to plant the gospel. Subsequent events altered Paul's manner of going to Rome (see Acts 21:17-28, 31). Luke records no visit to Spain, but putting together Paul's words in the pastoral epistles (1 and 2 Tim.; Titus), plus extrabiblical writings (see Clement's *Epistle to the Corinthians;* the *Muratorian Canon;* Moody, p. 277), it is likely that he did go there after his release from his first Roman imprisonment. "To be brought . . . thitherward by you" (v. 24) probably refers to letters of introduction and financial aid.

In verses 25-29 Paul mentions his trip to Jerusalem, and its purpose, before coming to Rome. He requests the prayers of the Roman Christians that he may have a safe visit to Judea, including deliverance from his Jewish enemies there, and that his ministry may be accepted by the saints of Jerusalem (vv. 30–31). This to the end that in joy he may come to Rome through God's will and that they with him may be refreshed (v. 32). He closes this account of his past ministry and projected plans with a benediction (v. 33).

Some see this as the end of the epistle, with chapter 16 being a later addition. However, this most probably is not the case. Paul had many friends in Rome even though he had never been there. It is not surprising that Christians whom he had known elsewhere would now be in Rome. However, except for personal matters, Paul's letter was finished with 15:33.

12

The Conclusion of Paul's Letter

Romans 16:1–27

As previously noted this chapter is largely personal in nature. For the most part Paul is saying hello to his various friends. It is interesting to see so carefully reasoned a letter ending on so personal a note. However, it is not unlike Paul who dearly loved his Christian brethren as he did his brethren in the flesh.

Paul's Commendation of Phoebe (16:1–2)

Scholarly opinion is divided almost equally as to the nature of these verses. Were they a note of recommendation of Phoebe (Greek, *Phoibēn;* KJV, Phebe) appended to this letter to Rome? Or was it a note sent about her to Ephesus? It is not my purpose to delve into this. However, I see it as a part of the text of Romans. Evidently she was the bearer of the letter, and this note was Paul's way of commending her and showing that the letter was genuine and not a forgery (see 2 Thess. 3:17).

"I commend unto you Phebe our sister, which is a servant of the church which is at Cenchrea" (v. 1).

"Commend" translates a Greek verb meaning to place together, to recommend to favorable attention, to vouch for. Moffatt reads, "Let me introduce our sister Phoebe."

Other than these two verses nothing is known about Phoebe, but she is presented as a faithful servant of the Lord. Her name means bright or radiant. She is described as a "sister" in the Christian sense and as "a servant of the church." Here "church" (*ekklēsia*) refers to the *local* church in Cenchreae, the eastern port for Corinth on the Saronic Gulf. This use of the church as a local body is found throughout this chapter (vv. 1, 4–5, 16, 23). Out of 115 times the word *ekklēsia* is used in the New Testament, at least 93 times it is used in the local sense. It is used at times to refer to the collective body of redeemed people as Christ's body (see Col. 1:24; Eph. 1:22–23; note Eph. 3:10). In Acts 19 it is translated "assembly" denoting a local political group in a free city in the Roman Empire (see v. 41).

"Servant" (*diakonon*) grammatically may be either masculine or feminine gender. Used of a woman it is feminine and may read "deaconess" (see RSV, Williams). Interpreters differ as to whether this should read a female servant or carries the official title such as "deacon." It is a disputed question today whether or not a church should have *deaconesses* along with *deacons.* Robertson (p. 425) holds that since the word is followed by "of the church" it should read "deaconess." Moody (p. 279) notes that deaconesses were prominent in the ancient church. Their duties probably consisted of tending the poor and sick, ministry to martyrs and confessors in prison, teaching catechumens, assisting in the baptism of women, ministering to women members, and providing hospitality for traveling Christians. In a port city this last would be important.

The church in Rome is asked to receive her in the Lord in a manner fitting for saints (v. 2) and also to lend whatever aid she needed. "Business" or practical matter may mean that she was going to Rome on an errand of business. She was deserving of help because she had helped many, including Paul himself. Whatever may be one's view of "deaconess," this is a beautiful portrait of a *radiant* woman. Paul has been labeled a woman-hater, but at least eight of the twenty-eight people mentioned in this chapter are women (Moody, p. 279).

Paul's Greetings to Friends (16:3–16)

In verse 3 Paul begins his series of greetings to his friends in Rome. He begins with Aquila and Priscilla (v. 3; see Acts 18:2–3) whom he first met in Corinth. Later they went to Ephesus (see Acts 18:24–26). Now that Jews were allowed back in Rome, they had returned after being expelled from there by Claudius in A.D. 49. Later they returned to Ephesus (see 2 Tim. 4:19). Wherever they went, they were busy for the Lord!

He rightly describes them as "my fellow-workers in Christ Jesus." They had for Paul's life "laid down their own necks" (v. 4), literally, "placed their own necks under," as under the axe. Figuratively, it probably refers to their risking their lives for Paul during the riot in Ephesus (see Acts 19:23–41). Probably they hid him in their home until he could escape the city. Both Paul and the Gentile churches were in their debt. He also greeted the church which met in their house (v. 5). Nothing is known of Ephaenetus (meaning praised) other than here. He evidently was the first convert in the Roman province of Asia, or Paul's first convert there.

Who the "Mary" is in verse 6 is not known. Some manuscripts read "Miriam" (Hebrew). She may have been a Jewish

Christian who had worked strenuously for the church in Rome.
The best texts read "you," not "us."

"Andronicus and Junia" (v. 7) were "kinsmen" of Paul, but
this probably means that they were fellow Jews according to the
flesh (see 9:13). They had been fellow prisoners with Paul in
one of his imprisonments (see 2 Cor. 6:5; 11:23) and had
labored with him in apostolic work. They were counted as apostles like Barnabas and Silas, and they had become Christians
prior to Paul's conversion.

Amplias, or Ampliatus, is an unknown (v. 8), but the name
Ampliati appears on the walls of a second-century Roman cata-
comb (Moody, p. 281). He may have been of that family. "Ur-
bane" means "city-bred," and "Stachys" means "an ear of grain"
(v. 9). "Apelles" is described as "approved" or tried and true in
Christ (v. 10).

Those of Aristobulus evidently refer to his slaves who had
become Christians. The same may be said of those of Narcissus
(v. 11). It has been suggested that this Aristobulus was a
brother of Herod Agrippa I and a private citizen in Rome. As
a friend of Claudius he may have bequeathed his slaves to him,
but they still would have been referred to as *Aristobuliani*, Latin
for Paul's phrase. The household of Narcissus has been identified as that of Tiberius Claudius. Narcissus was a wealthy freed-
man of the Emperor Tiberius who wielded great influence under
Claudius but was executed by order of Agrippina, Nero's mother
(Tacitus, *Annales*, 13:1; see Moody, p. 281). Had his slaves
been passed on to the emperor they would still bear his name.
Herodion (v. 11), who probably belonged to the Herod family,
was a fellow countryman of Paul.

Robertson (p. 428) suggests that Tryphena and Tryphosa
were twin sisters (v. 12). Their names mean *dainty* and *deli-
cate*. The root of their names (*truphaō*, James 5:5) means to
live luxuriously. The name of Persis suggests that she was of
Persian descent or from Persia. Since she "laboured" (past
tense) much in the Lord may mean that she was an aged
woman. "Beloved" is a translation of the Greek word for Christian love. This could mean that Paul loved her in the Lord
and/or that the church loved her.

"Rufus" was a common slave name (v. 13). F. F. Bruce suggests that he was the son of Simon of Cyrene (see Mark 15:21).
His name means "red head." His mother has shown maternal
care for Paul. Verses 14-15 include two groups of five each.
The five in verse 14 may have been slaves in a household, and
"the brethren" other Christians who joined them there or elsewhere for worship. Moody (p. 282) suggests that Philologus

and Julia may have been husband and wife and the other three their children (v. 15). "Salute one another with an holy kiss" (v. 16). Rabbis so greeted each other. The Christians took up this custom as men kissed men and women kissed women. It was something like our handshake. "The churches of Christ" were those churches in the eastern Mediterranean. The phrase then carried no sectarian meaning as some give it today.

Paul's Warning about False Teachers (16:17–20)

In between Paul's greetings and those of his associates the apostle injects this warning against false teachers. Interpreters agree that these were not Jews with their scruples about diet. However, it could be the Judaizers (see Acts 15:1) who had disrupted churches containing Gentile Christians, or it could be teachers of incipient Gnosticism against whom Paul later wrote in Colossians. At any rate, Paul told his readers to "mark" them (v. 17). The verb form (*skopeō*) means to keep the eye on the goal; so he says to keep their eyes on such or be on the lookout for such. A similar warning against Judaizers is issued in Philippians 3:2. The description of them in verse 18 suggests Gnostics with their dualism regarding matter and spirit.

At any rate these people were dividing churches and teaching contrary to the teaching about Christ that the Roman Christians had received. This, of course, could fit either Judaizers with their works (circumcision and living by the Mosaic law) plus faith rather than salvation by grace through faith. Or it could be the Gnostics whose treatment reduced Christ to a created being, a demigod and almost a demon, by saying that he possessed enough deity to create but so little as to create evil matter. There were two groups of Gnostics. One (Docetics) said that Christ did not have a real material body but only seemed to have. The other (Cerinthians) said that Christ was neither born nor did he die; deity came upon Jesus at his baptism and left him on the cross. The former denied Christ's humanity; the latter denied Jesus' deity. Those holding these positions today are not modern advanced thinkers. They are nothing more than Neo-Gnostics. Paul said to keep an eye on such and "avoid" or "bow them out" (*ekklinō, klinō*, to bow, *ek*, out). This advice holds today.

These people are deceptive. They do not serve "our Lord Christ" (Greek text) but their own stomachs (v. 18). They may pose as religious teachers, even claiming to have an advanced form of Christian teaching. Serving slavishly the "belly" probably is Paul's way of saying that they serve their own self-interests (see Phil. 3:19). By their "good words and fair speeches" they lead astray the "simple" or innocent, those without evil. "Good words" means fair speaking or smooth words which appear as goodness. "Fair speeches" (*eulogia*) denotes here polished language.

Paul rejoices over the Christians in Rome (v. 19) because the knowledge of their obedience "is come abroad." The Greek verb means to come from one place and arrive at another. The report of their obedience had arrived in Corinth as well as other places. Even so Paul adds his wish that they be wise with respect to the good and without guile with respect to the evil. He assures his readers that victory is theirs in the Lord (v. 20). The God of peace will trample under his feet Satan the adversary who works through these false teachers (see Gen. 3:15). It will be done "shortly." This is by God's time, not ours. In the meantime they are to be faithful to God. Paul closes this admonition with a brief benediction. "Christ" is not in the best texts.

Paul's Associates' Greetings (16:21–24)

After his own greetings and warning Paul adds the greetings of those with him in Corinth. Timothy was Paul's fellow worker (v. 21). His name means one who honors God, and he certainly had lived up to the name given him at birth. Lucius could be the one mentioned in Acts 13:1, or he could even be Luke, Paul's traveling companion and physician (see Col. 4:14). Jason probably is the man who was Paul's host in Thessalonica (see Acts 17:5–9). Also Sosipater could be Sopater of Berea (see Acts 20:4), but one cannot be certain. They are all three Paul's countrymen.

Tertius was the amanuensis (writer) as Paul dictated the letter (v. 22). "I Tertius" shows that he himself inserted his greeting. "In the Lord" stresses that he was a Christian. It is possible that he was a Roman since his name is Latin for *third*. He evidently thought that Paul had finished these greetings, but he added three more. "Gaius" was baptized by Paul in Corinth (see 1 Cor. 1:14). Since he is described as Paul's host in Corinth, he may be identified with Titius (Greek text) Justus of Acts 18:7. If so, his full name would be Gaius Titius Justus. As a Roman citizen in Corinth he would have three names (praenomen, nomen, cognomen, see Moody, p. 285).

Erastus is identified as "the chamberlain of the city." "Chamberlain" translates a Greek word meaning "house manager." It may also read "steward" (see 1 Cor. 4:1–2). The word is variously translated here: Denney, city treasurer (see ASV); Vincent, administrator of the city lands; Robertson, city treasurer or city manager, probably the administrator of the city's property.

A marble paving block, dated about A.D. 50–100, has been discovered in old Corinth, bearing the inscription: "Erastus, commissioner for public works, laid this pavement at his own expense." Moody says, "The only major problem is that the commissioner for public works is not the city treasurer, but Bruce thinks he got a promotion before Paul came" (p. 285). At any rate this shows a Christian of public prominence in Corinth.

Quartus is simply identified as "the brother." "The brother" could mean "my brother." He was certainly a Christian *brother*, but why is he alone so designated? It could be that he is the younger brother of Tertius who wrote Paul's words in Romans. Tertius means "third." Quartus means "fourth." Roman sons were sometimes given the name which denoted the order of their birth (see "Secundus," second, Acts 20:4). The best texts do not have verse 24.

Paul's Closing Doxology (16:25–27)

Robertson calls this "the finest of Paul's doxologies" (p. 430). It is fitting that it should close so wonderful a book.

The doxology is addressed to God who is able to establish Paul's readers "according to my gospel, and the preaching of Jesus Christ" or about Jesus Christ (v. 25). "My gospel" refers to the gospel as preached by Paul and set forth in this letter. "Preaching" is that which is proclaimed about Jesus Christ. It is the revelation of the "mystery" of God's redemptive purpose which was "fully kept in silence" (perfect tense) through times of the ages, but it is now manifested or made plain through the prophetic Scriptures. It was witnessed by the law and the prophets (Old Testament), a fact that runs throughout Romans (v. 26). This was according to the command of the eternal God, with a view to obedience of faith, being made known to all nations.

"To God only wise, be glory through Jesus Christ for ever," or "unto the ages of the ages, Amen" (v. 27). "Unto the ages of the ages" is the strongest Greek phrase for eternity.

Sometime shortly after writing this letter Paul departed for Jerusalem for unanticipated experiences which awaited him there. Perhaps Phoebe had already departed for Rome on her errand of personal business. Little could she realize how much she was on the King's business. For as she went she "carried under the folds of her robe the whole future of Christian theology" (Ernest Renan, *The Life of Jesus*).

Bibliography

Archer, Gleason L., Jr. *The Epistle to the Romans.* Grand Rapids, Mich.: Baker Book House, 1959.

Barclay, William. *The Letter to the Romans.* Rev. ed. Philadelphia: Westminster Press, 1975.

Bruce, F. F. *The Epistle of Paul to the Romans.* Grand Rapids, Mich.: Wm. B. Eerdmans, 1963.

Denney, James. *St. Paul's Epistle to the Romans.* The Expositor's Greek Testament. Vol. 2. Edited by W. Robertson Nicoll. Grand Rapids, Mich.: Wm B. Eerdmans, 1951.

Lloyd-Jones, D. Martin. *Romans.* Vol. 2, *Assurance.* Exposition of Chapter 5. Grand Rapids, Mich.: Zondervan, 1971

Moody, Dale. *Romans.* Broadman Bible Commentary. Nashville: Broadman Press, 1970.

Robertson, Archibald Thomas. *Word Pictures in the New Testament.* Vol. 4. New York: Richard R. Smith, 1931.

Scott, E. F. *Paul's Epistle to the Romans.* London: S.C.M. Press, 1947.

Vincent, Marvin. *Word Studies in the New Testament.* 4 volumes. Grand Rapids, Mich.: Wm. B. Eerdmans, 1957.

Wuest, Kenneth S. *Word Studies in the Greek New Testament.* Vol. 16, *Romans.* Grand Rapids, Mich.: Wm. B. Eerdmans, 1955.